CONTENTS

First published in 1998 by MBI Publishing Company, 729 Prospect Avenue, PO Box 1, Osceola, WI 54020-0001 USA

MBI Publishing Company books are also available at discounts in bulk quantity for industrial or sales-promotional use.
For details write to Special Sales Manager at
Motorbooks International Wholesalers & Distributors, 729 Prospect Avenue, PO Box 1, Osceola, WI 54020-0001 USA.

Edited by: Lee Klancher • Designed by: Rebecca Allen

Printed in Hong Kong   ISBN 0-7603-0597-8

Thank you Race Fans for your support of the 1998 Brickyard 400, the largest and most successful of the five events we have had with NASCAR. Four days of generally good weather, our first International Race of Champions (IROC) and a fast, competitive Brickyard 400 made for a great week.

Mark Martin and Jeff Gordon shared the spotlight, with Mark capturing the IROC race and IROC season championship, and Jeff winning his second Brickyard 400. Jeff Gordon also became the first to win the Winston No Bull Million which combined with his winner's purse gave him the largest payday in racing history, continuing that record being held at the Indianapolis Motor Speedway.

The real stars of the week were the fans that turned out in record numbers for the four days of the Brickyard. Your enthusiasm for the race and the racers is what this sport is all about.

Thank you again for your support of the Indianapolis Motor Speedway and its events, and we look forward to seeing you again next year.

Tony George

NASCAR®
Comes to Indy®

Hometown Hero Jeff Gordon Makes His Mark *by Al Pearce*

It's hard to imagine anyone writing a better script for the inaugural Brickyard 400, which took place on the first Saturday in August 1994. The historic stock car race consisted of everything that makes a good yarn memorable—an enormous, well-conceived build-up, a spirited story line from start to finish, dramatic twists and turns down the stretch, and a fairy tale ending that left almost everyone itching for more. Indeed, the venerable Indianapolis Motor Speedway hadn't seen anything like it in years.

The first NASCAR race at the world's most famous motorsports venue came after years of talk and wishful speculation. From either well on high or from deep below—there are those who swear by both—NASCAR's deceased founder Bill France Sr. and the late Indianapolis Motor Speedway president Tony Hulman must have been looking on with great interest and pride. They might also have had more than just a little concern that the great experiment of their heirs might fall short of expectations.

For years, there had been talk that NASCAR might bring its Winston Cup teams to Indianapolis, even though France and Hulman

A NASCAR-record 300,000-plus gathered on the first Saturday in August of 1994 for the long-awaited Brickyard 400. The race helped introduce tens of thousands of Indy loyalists from the Midwest to the color, competition, and excitement of Winston Cup stock car racing.

BRICKYARD 400 • INAUGURAL RACE
AUGUST 6, 1994

5

Left

It was a magical homecoming weekend for Jeff Gordon, the local favorite from nearby Pittsboro, Indiana. After qualifying third in the No. 24 Dupont Chevrolet Lumina, he raced near the front all afternoon. In the waning laps, when leader Ernie Irvan slowed with a flat tire, Gordon drove by in dramatic fashion to win the first stock car race at the Indianapolis Motor Speedway.

had never been especially close. In the mid-1950s, in fact, one of Hulman's well-meaning lieutenants had France unceremoniously removed from the Speedway's garage area during preparations for the Indianapolis 500. Hulman later apologized and said it was all an unfortunate mistake, but France was never known as one who easily forgave or quickly forgot.

There's no evidence that similar friction has ever existed between Tony George, grandson of the Speedway's long-time owner, and Bill France Jr., eldest son of the NASCAR founder. And it certainly didn't hurt matters that respected motorsports executive John Cooper once served as president of both the Daytona International Speedway and the Indianapolis Motor Speedway. As much as anyone, he made the first steps toward what eventually became the Brickyard 400.

Even so, the race was more than a year in the making. In April 1993, with most of the world's motorsports community looking on, France Jr. and George hosted a long-anticipated press conference in Indianapolis. George spoke of the speedway's 80 years of tradition, and France addressed the unprecedented 10-year growth spurt of Winston Cup racing. Each agreed that a stock car race at the Indianapolis Motor Speedway (IMS) was the right thing to do for the most basic reasons: It would attract a sellout crowd of almost 300,000, generate enormous revenue

THE 1992 TEST

More than 20,000 fans showed up at the Indianapolis Motor Speedway on a Monday morning in June 1992 to watch the first open test of NASCAR stock cars at the world's most famous track. The 10 teams invited to the test came directly from the previous day's 400-mile Winston Cup race in Brooklyn, Michigan.

Even though journeyman racer H. B. Bailey didn't make the field, he earned a place in Indianapolis Motor Speedway history by being the first driver to make a qualifying attempt for the inaugural Brickyard 400. Neither of his attempts in a Pontiac Grand Prix were fast enough to make the 43-car field—he was first in line for Round 1, then last in line on the second day.

Pennzoil has been among the major sponsors of the Brickyard 400 and was rewarded for its support in the inaugural race. Michael Waltrip qualified the Pennzoil No. 30 Pontiac Grand Prix 15th, then finished a lead-lap 8th (two positions behind his older brother, Darrell) for long-time team owners Chuck Rider and Lowrance Harry.

Brett Bodine played a major role in the first Brickyard 400. His controversial Turn 4 accident with his older brother, Geoff, at Lap 99 eliminated the cars of Geoff Bodine and Dale Jarrett and damaged several others. Brett soldiered on to finish second and earn a career-best $203,575 for himself and team owner Kenny Bernstein.

THE 1993 TEST

In the summer of 1993, shortly after IMS president Tony George and NASCAR president Bill France confirmed the date for the inaugural Brickyard 400, NASCAR conducted another open test session at the Indianapolis Motor Speedway. Most of the top Winston Cup teams were there for the three-day test.

The Ray Evernham-led "Rainbow Warriors" gave No. 3 starter and eventual race-winner Jeff Gordon quick and precise service throughout the 1994 Brickyard 400. Even so, Gordon likely would have finished second if Ernie Irvan hadn't cut a tire and slowed while leading at Lap 156.

One of the most popular drivers in the 1994 Brickyard 400 was Missouri native Ken Schrader, part of the three-team Hendrick Motorsports organization. He had a huge fan following at the Indianapolis Motor Speedway, a following built largely through his years of running sprint car, midget, and dirt-track races at backwater tracks throughout the Midwest.

Three-time NASCAR champion Darrell Waltrip wasn't a serious contender in the first Brickyard 400, but smart race driving moved him from 27th on the grid to 6th at the end. In a Chevrolet Lumina, he was one of 16 drivers on the lead lap after 160 laps around the Indianapolis Motor Speedway.

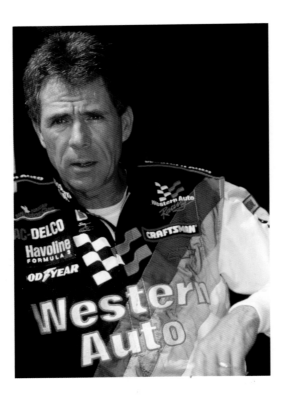

for all concerned, and enhance the world-wide reputation of both NASCAR and the Speedway.

Right from the start, it was clear that nobody would confuse the Brickyard 400 with the annual Memorial Day weekend Indianapolis 500. The stock car race would be shorter by 40 laps (160 instead of 200) and 100 miles less than the Indianapolis 500. It would be run on the first Saturday during the heat of August, with Sunday as a built-in rain date. Instead of 11 rows of cars aligned three-wide, the Brickyard 400 grid would have 21 rows of cars side-by-side. However, like the Indy 500, which had thrived all its life without a title sponsor, the new NASCAR race would also stand alone, as the Brickyard 400.

Tickets would go on sale, George said during the press conference, sometime in the middle of the summer. The Speedway still had the 1993 Indianapolis 500 to run, and George and his staff would have their hands full with that. There would be no more official announcements about the 1994 Brickyard 400 until after the upcoming Indy 500; the race was, after all, more than 16 months in the future.

With political clouds gathering on the horizon, George knew he'd soon be battling the hierarchy at Championship Auto Racing Teams (CART) for control of the Indy car racing world. He knew there might be a day when he would need to create a renegade sanctioning body. And that would undoubtedly cost him the support of Indy-car racing's biggest guns and brightest stars. Having a Winston Cup race at the Speedway would help ease the pain if CART kept most of its stars away from the Indianapolis 500.

Pole-sitter Rick Mast (No. 1 Ford Thunderbird) held off a determined bid from second-starting Dale Earnhardt (in the No. 3 Chevrolet Lumina) and led the first two laps of the 1994 race. Mast withstood not only Earnhardt's bid to lead early but that of No. 7 Ford Thunderbird driver Geoff Bodine as well.

Left
Rusty Wallace started 12th in the 1994 race but quickly came toward the front. He was a strong runner all afternoon, leading laps 132–135 during an exchange of pits stops and finishing a lead-lap 4th behind winner Jeff Gordon, runner-up Brett Bodine, and 3rd-place driver Bill Elliott.

9

Hardly a moment went by during the 1994 race weekend that local hero Jeff Gordon and crew chief Ray Evernham weren't besieged by fans, the media, and assorted autograph hunters. They accommodated as many as they could but never lost focus of why they were in Indianapolis in the first place.

Former Winston Cup champion Bill Elliott started 6th, led a lap, and finished a lead-lap 4th in the 1994 race. He's the only driver to have completed all 160 laps in each of the five events: he placed 4th in the first race, 5th in the second, 10th in the third, 8th in the 1997 race, and 12th in 1998.

The popular "Skoal Bandit" team featuring Harry Gant had an eventful 400. It took one of two available provisionals just to make the field, saw its driver race into the lead at lap 47, then lost 27 laps making mid-race engine repairs. Gant finished 37th in his first and only Indianapolis Motor Speedway appearance.

As 1993 turned into 1994, neither George nor France nor the American racing public could have guessed what was coming the first week in August—although they did get a hint when more than a quarter of a million Brickyard 400 tickets were gobbled up within days of going on sale. There was also an unprecedented deluge of credential requests from the worldwide media, many of whom had never deigned to staff a NASCAR race. And when corporate America queued up to throw its support behind the Brickyard 400, it became abundantly clear this wouldn't be just another superspeedway stock car race. Jeff Gordon and his No. 24 Hendrick Motorsports Chevrolet Monte Carlo saw to that.

Gordon started third, ran up front all afternoon, and made a late-race pass of Ernie Irvan to win the 400. Several hours later—as all of Indiana was talking about what its adopted "native son" had done—Gordon and his wife, Brooke, were munching on pizza and watching ABC's replay of the race at the Speedway Motel. "It had been a long day," Gordon said later. "We really didn't feel much like going out."

The historic weekend began on Thursday, when H. B. Bailey became the first driver to make an official NASCAR qualifying lap around the IMS. The fact that he didn't crack the top-25 the first day or make the field in the second qualifying session was a bittersweet disappointment. But the native Texan went back home knowing his place in IMS history was secure. While Mike Wallace may have been the first driver on the track when it opened for practice Wednesday, it was Bailey who went into the history books.

Rick Mast won the pole and led the first two laps to become the answer to another trivia question. By the end of the race, a dozen other drivers had swapped the lead 21 times. They included Gordon, Irvan, all three of the Bodine brothers—Geoff, Brett, and Todd—Greg Sacks, Dale Earnhardt, Ted Musgrave, Lake Speed, Harry Gant, and Rusty Wallace. But Gordon was clearly the class of the field, leading seven times for 93 of the 160 laps. The only other drivers to lead more than one time were Geoff Bodine (twice for 24 laps) and Irvan (twice for 11 laps).

After starting 17th, Irvan relentlessly worked his way toward the front. He became a serious contender when he caught Rusty Wallace and wrestled away the lead for the first time at Lap 140. He led for five laps, yielded to Gordon for the next five, then powered back into the lead at Lap 150. He seemed to have the race well in-hand until his luck ran out. His Robert Yates-owned No. 28 Ford Thunderbird cut down a right-front tire and began to slow with six laps remaining. Gordon had no trouble driving past and went on to beat Brett Bodine by slightly more than a half-second. Bill Elliott, Rusty Wallace, and Dale Earnhardt rounded out the top five.

As for Ernie Irvan—he lost a lap with a late-race pit stop and finished 17th, exactly where he'd started 3 hours, 1 minute, and 51 seconds earlier. Instead of winning about $600,000, he had to be content with $52,000. But at least his car was in one piece. Six others—those of Jimmy Spencer, Mike Chase, Dave Marcis, Dale Jarrett, Geoff Bodine, and Geoff Brabham—went to the garage because of accidents. Hut Stricklin

Four-time Indy 500 winner A. J. Foyt "unretired" and surprised everyone—except, perhaps, himself—by qualifying 40th for the inaugural Brickyard 400. He hustled his Ford Thunderbird from deep on the grid to 2nd place by Lap 47 but ran out of gas and lost several laps. He eventually finished 30th, four laps down but running at the end.

was an oil line-related DNF, and Harry Gant limped home 27 laps behind after his crew had to spend time in the garage working on their Chevrolet engine.

The day's most controversial accident—indeed, one of the year's most unusual—involved Geoff and Brett Bodine. It began innocently enough when Geoff gave his younger brother a minor but effective tap as he passed for position going into Turn 3 on Lap 99. Moments later, Brett returned the favor, bumping his brother exiting Turn 4. But unlike the first incident—which, in truth, was relatively harmless—the second caused Geoff Bodine to spin

Dale Earnhardt started the No. 3 Chevrolet Lumina from the outside of the front row but led only two laps (38–39) en route to a solid fifth-place finish for owner Richard Childress and long-time sponsor Goodwrench.

Ernie Irvan seemingly had the inaugural Brickyard 400 won until cutting a left-side tire and slowing to a 17th-place finish in the finals laps. He qualified only 17th but ran well enough to lead laps 140–145, then again from 150 until 156 when his No. 28 Ford Thunderbird abruptly slowed in Turns 1 and 2.

amidst heavy traffic. When the smoke cleared and the damage was assessed, not only was Geoff sidelined for the day, but Jarrett as well.

A few minutes later, Geoff Bodine was telling anyone who would listen that the bump from his brother was intentional (a claim Brett later called "ridiculous"), and that it was part of an on-going family feud. "He's still my little brother, and I love him," he said of Brett, "but he wrecked me. He brought something that doesn't belong on the track to the race, and that's bad. We've been having some problems within the family, and he took it out on me·over in Turn 4."

Emotions ran high, as well, for the victorious Gordon and his family. He had grown up in Pittsboro, Indiana, just west of Indianapolis, and spent his formative years in open-wheel, open-cockpit cars at nearby Indianapolis Raceway Park. "I always dreamed of winning at this speedway," he said, "but I never thought I'd get a chance when I went to NASCAR instead of Indy cars. This is amazing, to win the first NASCAR race at a place that has all this tradition and history. This is something else, I'll tell you that."

And, indeed, it certainly was.

John Andretti was one of four drivers—the others were A. J. Foyt, Geoff Brabham, and Danny Sullivan—to make Indianapolis Motor Speedway history in the 1994 Brickyard 400. They were the only drivers to have raced in an Indianapolis 500 and Brickyard 400, although Andretti was the only one to have done them both in the same year. Andretti started 28th and finished 28th—two laps behind—in a Chevrolet Lumina owned by Billy Hagan and sponsored by Bryant Heating and Cooling.

OFFICIAL BOX SCORE

Inaugural Brickyard 400–August 6, 1994
Indianapolis Motor Speedway • NASCAR Winston Cup Series

FP	SP	Car	Driver	Car Name & Brand	Laps Comp	Running/ Reason	Prize Money
1	3	24	Jeff Gordon	94 DuPont Chevrolet	160	131.932	$613,000
2	7	26	Brett Bodine	94 Quaker State Ford	160	Running	$203,575
3	6	11	Bill Elliott	94 Budweiser/Amoco Ford	160	Running	$164,850
4	12	2	Rusty Wallace	94 Miller Genuine Draft Ford	160	Running	$140,600
5	2	3	Dale Earnhardt	94 GM Goodwrench Service Chevrolet	160	Running	$121,625
6	27	17	Darrell Waltrip	94 Western Auto Chevrolet	160	Running	$82,600
7	23	25	Ken Schrader	94 Kodiak Chevrolet	160	Running	$77,400
8	15	30	Michael Waltrip	94 Pennzoil Pontiac	160	Running	$72,300
9	25	75	Todd Bodine	94 Factory Stores of America Ford	160	Running	$63,600
10	11	21	Morgan Shepherd	94 Citgo Petroleum Ford	160	Running	$67,350
11	8	10	Ricky Rudd	94 Tide Ford	160	Running	$57,100
12	21	5	Terry Labonte	94 Kellogg's Chevrolet	160	Running	$57,500
13	37	16	Ted Musgrave	94 Family Channel Ford	160	Running	$52,800
14	9	4	Sterling Marlin	94 Kodak Chevrolet	160	Running	$49,000
15	41	15	Lake Speed	94 Quality Care Ford	160	Running	$52,350
16	5	22	Bobby Labonte	94 Maxwell House Coffee Pontiac	160	Running	$43,800
17	17	28	Ernie Irvan	94 Texaco/Havoline Ford	159	Running	$52,000
18	13	77	Greg Sacks	94 USAir/Jasper Engines Ford	159	Running	$39,300
19	38	8	Jeff Burton	94 Raybestos Douglas Ford	159	Running	$41,600
20	30	41	Joe Nemechek	94 Meineke Muffler Chevrolet	159	Running	$36,650
21	35	44	Bobby Hillin	94 Buss Fuses Ford	159	Running	$32,000
22	1	1	Rick Mast	94 Big Foot/Skoal Racing Ford	159	Running	$103,200
23	22	43	Wally Dallenbach Jr.	94 STP Pontiac	159	Running	$32,300
24	32	40	Bobby Hamilton	94 Kendall Oil Pontiac	159	Running	$35,200
25	36	42	Kyle Petty	94 Mello Yello Kendall Uniden Pontiac	159	Running	$39,000
26	31	98	Jeremy Mayfield	94 Fingerhut Ford	158	Running	$29,100
27	39	02	Derrike Cope	94 Children's Miracle Network Ford	158	Running	$26,000
28	28	14	John Andretti	94 Bryant/Byrd's Cafeteria Chevrolet	158	Running	$39,000
29	19	9	Rich Bickle	94 Orkin Pest Control Ford	157	Running	$24,000
30	40	50	A. J. Foyt	94 Copenhagen Ford	156	Running	$29,000
31	33	31	Ward Burton	94 Hardee's Chevrolet	155	Running	$23,500
32	24	55	Jimmy Hensley	94 Bondo/Mar-Hyde Ford	155	Running	$23,000
33	26	99	Danny Sullivan	94 Corporate Car of Indy Chevrolet	152	Running	$22,750
34	29	51	Jeff Purvis	94 Country Time Chevy	142	Running	$22,500
35	10	6	Mark Martin	94 Valvoline/Reese's Ford	140	Running	$34,300
36	20	23	Hut Stricklin	94 Camel Cigarettes Ford	136	Oil Line	$24,000
37	42	33	Harry Gant	94 Gas America/Skoal Bandit Chevrolet	133	Running	$58,350
38	18	07	Geoff Brabham	94 Kmart Ford	127	Accident	$27,400
39	4	7	Geoff Bodine	94 Exide Batteries Ford	99	Accident	$45,600
40	14	18	Dale Jarrett	94 Interstate Batteries Chevrolet	99	Accident	$33,225
41	16	71	Dave Marcis	94 Terramite Const. Equip. Chevrolet	92	Accident	$21,825
42	43	58	Mike Chase	94 Tyson Foods Chevrolet	91	Accident	$21,825
43	34	27	Jimmy Spencer	94 McDonald's Ford	9	Accident	$21,825

Total Posted Awards — $3,213,849

Legend: SP = Starting Position, FP = Finishing Position, # = Rookie • **Time of Race:** 3:01:51
Average Speed: 131.932 mph • **Margin of Victory:** 0.53 second • **Fastest Lap:** #24 Jeff Gordon, Lap 68, 170.674 mph

Lap Leaders*

1–2	#1 Rick Mast
3–24	#24 Jeff Gordon
25–33	#7 Geoff Bodine
34–34	#11 Bill Elliott
35–35	#75 Todd Bodine
36–37	#77 Greg Sacks
38–39	#3 Dale Earnhardt
40–41	#16 Ted Musgrave
42–46	#15 Lake Speed
47–47	#33 Harry Gant
48–70	#24 Jeff Gordon
71–72	#77 Greg Sacks
73–80	#24 Jeff Gordon

Lap Leaders* (cont.)

81–95	#7 Geoff Bodine
96–105	#26 Brett Bodine
106–131	#24 Jeff Gordon
132–135	#2 Rusty Wallace
136–139	#24 Jeff Gordon
140–144	#28 Ernie Irvan
145–149	#24 Jeff Gordon
150–155	#28 Ernie Irvan
156–160	#24 Jeff Gordon

* 21 lead changes between 13 drivers
** Number of times in lead/number of laps led

Lap Leader Recap**

Jeff Gordon	7/93
Geoff Bodine	2/24
Ernie Irvan	2/11
Brett Bodine	1/10
Lake Speed	1/5
Greg Sacks	2/4
Rusty Wallace	1/4
Ted Musgrave	1/2
Rick Mast	1/2
Dale Earnhardt	1/2
Todd Bodine	1/1
Bill Elliott	1/1
Harry Gant	1/1

Caution Flags (6 for 25 laps)

Laps	Reason
4–5	Debris
12–15	Spencer hit Turn 3 wall
81–85	Debris Turn 4
95–99	Chase/Marcis accident
101–105	G. Bodine/Jarrett accident
131–134	Hensley/Brabham accident

BRICKYARD 400

INDIANAPOLIS MOTOR SPEEDWAY

AUGUST 5, 1995 ™

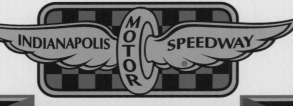

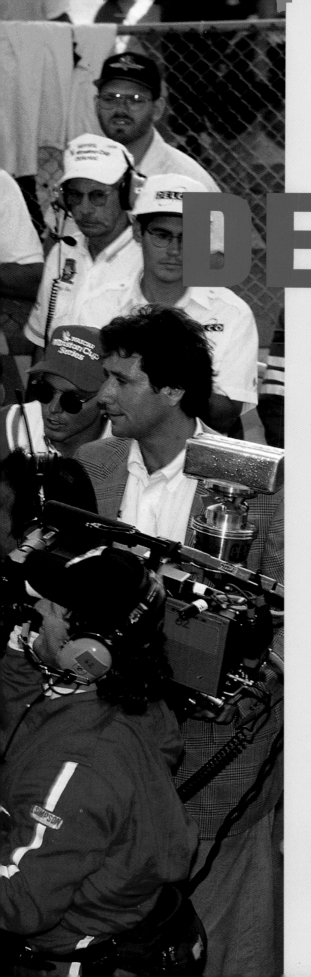

The Intimidator DELIVERS

Quick Pit Work Puts Earnhardt Past Wallace

by Al Pearce

For much of August 5, 1995, it looked like the second annual Brickyard 400 would have to be postponed. Gray skies and persistent rain greeted teams and race fans, and weather-watching locals said the dank drizzle looked to be settling in for the day. The National Weather Service wasn't hopeful, issuing a Saturday forecast for rain throughout the day—heavy at times—with temperatures in the upper 70s. In addition, it said any breaks would probably come late in the afternoon and be too short to allow the track to dry.

While NASCAR and speedway officials were not optimistic, they went through the pre-race motions as if conditions were perfect. The drivers' meeting was held on time, and ABC-TV came on the air promptly at 11 A.M. All told, the network had 21 cameras around the track, in cars, and on the Goodyear blimp overhead. As the aggravating rain delay grew longer, ABC had no choice but to yield to ESPN and switch to alternate programming. By the time the weather forecasters were proved wrong, it was too late for ABC to return for a live broadcast.

Ironically, conditions began improving about an hour after the race ordinarily would

After winning almost every other meaningful NASCAR race in his career (although he'd have to wait until 1998 for his precious first Daytona 500 victory), seven-time champion Dale Earnhardt added a gold star to his resume with a victory in the 1995 Brickyard 400.

BRICKYARD 400
AUGUST 5, 1995

Jeff Gordon, winner of the inaugural Brickyard 400, won the pole for the second annual race and led more laps than everyone except Bill Elliott. But the handling on his No. 24 Chevrolet Monte Carlo faded slightly toward the end, and he finished a lead-lap sixth.

Persistent rain in the Indianapolis area washed out the second qualifying session for the 1995 Brickyard 400. That forced NASCAR officials to take the fastest 38 from the first session on Thursday and add three provisionals based on owner points to fill the 41-car grid. Among the drivers who didn't get a second chance to qualify because of the rain: four-time Indy 500 winner A. J. Foyt and Winston Cup tour regulars Mike Wallace, Dave Marcis, and Billy Standridge.

have ended. Optimism became the prevailing mood as safety vehicles went out to dry the 2.5-mile track shortly before 3 P.M. Tens of thousands of fans out in the parking lot (and the handful of reporters who had given up and gone back to their hotels) rushed back to IMS when they heard via radio and TV bulletins that the race was on. Drivers went to their cars at 3:55, and the command from Mary Fendrich Hulman to start engines came 20 minutes later. The second annual Brickyard 400 took the green flag at 4:25, slightly more than 4 hours behind schedule.

It was well worth the wait. Pole-sitter and defending Brickyard 400 champion Jeff Gordon led the opening 31 laps (and 35 altogether), the first of 11 drivers who swapped the lead 17 times. Bill Elliott (47 laps), Dale Earnhardt (28), Rusty Wallace (22), Sterling Marlin (15), John Andretti (6), Bobby Labonte (2),

Ken Schrader (2), Bobby Hamilton (1), Bobby Hillin Jr. (1), and Michael Waltrip (1) also led, making the 1995 race one of the most entertaining and competitive of the season. Jeff Burton's single-car spin in Turn 2 at Lap 133 brought out the day's only caution period.

Much of the day belonged to Rusty Wallace, who started 24th but quickly cut his way up through traffic. He gained nine spots in the first 10 laps, five more positions in the next 20 laps, then took the lead for the first time in Laps 70 and 71. He stayed among the top five until pitting for gas and tires at Lap 97 in a green-flag stop that left him ninth. However, he powered back into the lead 12 laps later by passing Gordon, whose car was beginning to fade. Wallace built his lead to as much as 3.2 seconds before losing the lead—and, as it turned out, the race—because of an unfortunate incident on pit row.

Earnhardt, who started his Chevrolet Monte Carlo 13th and quietly loitered among the top five, was running 2nd when he made his final green-flag stop. It came at Lap 128, and he needed just 18 seconds to take four tires and gas. Wallace pitted at the same time for four tires and gas but lost precious seconds by having to slow up when Rich Bickle

After a rain delay of 4 hours and 10 minutes, the second annual Brickyard 400 began at 4:25 P.M. when pole-sitter Jeff Gordon in a Chevrolet and second-place qualifier Bobby Hamilton in a Pontiac took the green flag.

Two-time Daytona 500 winner Sterling Marlin started third, ran among the top 10 all afternoon, led once for 15 laps, and finished a lead-lap seventh.

and Joe Nemechek banged together ahead of him on his exit from the pits. By the time Rusty Wallace zigged to miss them and zagged to miss a tire rolling across his path, he had lost the lead to Earnhardt.

Hamilton (129) and Andretti (130–132) briefly led until cycling around for their final scheduled pit stops. By the time all service was completed, Earnhardt was ahead to stay. He never could shake Wallace—his advantage was never more than a half-second over the final 20 laps—but he was never seriously challenged either. In the end, the seven-time Winston Cup champion beat Wallace by nearly half a second, with Dale Jarrett almost a second behind. Elliott and Mark Martin rounded out the top-five when the race ended a minute before 7 P.M.

Thirty-six of the 41 starters were running at the finish, an event-record 19 of them on the lead lap. Engine problems sidelined the cars of Elton Sawyer, Derrike Cope, Bobby Hillin Jr., Ward Burton, and Bickle. The only

significant sheet metal damage was to the car of Jeff Burton, who slightly dented the front of his Ford when he spun at Lap 133 for the only caution.

In Earnhardt's mind, Wallace's pit road misfortune was the difference between the winner's circle and second place. And once Earnhardt saw the opening, he seized it like a pit bull on a steak. "That last pit stop was the key," he said after winning $645,000 for the Richard Childress Racing team. "Rusty had gotten behind in the pits and had to work his way out of traffic. I was in front, so I could run my consistent line and not worry about trying to pass anybody. My car ran really good once I got in front and was in clean air. It was important to stay in front because my car handled so much better with nobody ahead of me. When I was close behind somebody trying to pass, my car pushed pretty bad."

Earnhardt isn't known for being emotional, which made some of his post-race comments

Top
Rusty Wallace charged from 24th on the grid to finish a lead-lap 2nd, a bare one-third of a second behind Dale Earnhardt. After leading twice for 22 laps, Wallace was caught up in a brief pit road *contretemps* that cost him the lead—and, as it turned out—the race victory.

Efficient pit service from crew chief Steve Hmiel and the Roush Racing/Valvoline crew helped Mark Martin come from 14th on the grid to finish a lead-lap 6th in the 1995 Brickyard 400.

Above
The famous (infamous?) No. 3 Chevrolet Monte Carlo of Dale Earnhardt started 13th, ran among the top 10 all afternoon, then led the final 28 laps to win the 1995 Brickyard 400.

Right
Bill Elliott started fourth and led the most laps (three times for 47 laps), finishing a lead-lap fourth. He might have fared better if the brake pedal on his Ford Thunderbird hadn't started sticking to the floor when he was leading shortly after the race's halfway point.

The No. 30 Pontiac of Michael Waltrip leaves the pits as the Andy Petree-led crew of owner Richard Childress services the No. 3 Chevrolet of eventual winner Dale Earnhardt.

No. 4 starter Bill Elliott led the most laps in the second annual Brickyard 400—three times for 47 laps—on his way to finishing fourth. Here, he leads the No. 28 Ford of Dale Jarrett and the No. 31 Chevrolet of Ward Burton.

all the more memorable. "We didn't do any testing up here, so it's phenomenal to bring a new car here and win like this," he said. "To come up here and run is quite an honor, but to be a Brickyard 400 winner is pretty impressive. It doesn't make up for not having won a Daytona 500, but it's still probably up there with the biggest wins, if not THE biggest. It's the biggest of the day and the week. It's even probably the biggest of the month and the year. This is a tremendous feeling."

Wallace took the loss well but couldn't resist mentioning the costly pit road incident that put Earnhardt in front for good. "It's tough to lead that much (22 laps), then get blocked on pit road and lose the race," he said. "That hurt me because track position is real important here. We're not lacking in anything—performance, driving, or pit stops. It's just that I didn't count on the accident in the pits."

On such fine lines are races won and lost.

The end of a long rain-plagued day at the Indianapolis Motor Speedway: the crew for Rick Mast loads their Ford Thunderbird for the trip back to North Carolina after a solid eighth-place run in the 1995 Brickyard 400.

Right
The No. 3 Goodwrench Chevrolet crew celebrates Dale Earnhardt's 1995 Brickyard 400 victory as the early August sun begins slipping behind the Turn 1 grandstand of the Indianapolis Motor Speedway.

OFFICIAL BOX SCORE

Second Annual Brickyard 400–August 5, 1995
Indianapolis Motor Speedway • NASCAR Winston Cup Series

FP	SP	Car	Driver	Car Name & Brand	Laps Comp	Running/Reason	Prize Money
1	13	3	Dale Earnhardt	GM Goodwrench Service Plus Chevrolet	160	155.218	$565,600
2	24	2	Rusty Wallace	Miller Genuine Draft Ford	160	Running	$250,500
3	26	28	Dale Jarrett	Texaco/Havoline Ford	160	Running	$203,200
4	4	94	Bill Elliott	McDonald's Ford	160	Running	$223,450
5	14	6	Mark Martin	Valvoline Ford	160	Running	$144,850
6	1	24	Jeff Gordon	DuPont Auto Finishes Chevrolet	160	Running	$299,200
7	3	4	Sterling Marlin	Kodak Film Chevrolet	160	Running	$119,700
8	9	1	Rick Mast	Skoal Racing Ford	160	Running	$100,700
9	5	18	Bobby Labonte	Interstate Batteries Chevrolet	160	Running	$99,500
10	33	21	Morgan Shepherd	Citgo Ford	160	Running	$94,000
11	2	43	Bobby Hamilton	STP Pontiac	160	Running	$89,000
12	23	37	John Andretti	Kmart/Little Caesars Ford	160	Running	$77,400
13	15	5	Terry Labonte	Kellogg's Chevrolet	160	Running	$80,550
14	7	30	Michael Waltrip	Pennzoil Pontiac	160	Running	$74,300
15	25	7	Geoff Bodine	Exide Batteries Ford	160	Running	$79,400
16	19	16	Ted Musgrave	Family Channel Ford	160	Running	$71,800
17	20	17	Darrell Waltrip	Western Auto Chevrolet	160	Running	$70,700
18	11	15	Dick Trickle	Quality Care Ford	160	Running	$69,500
19	10	25	Ken Schrader	Budweiser Chevrolet	160	Running	$69,200
20	22	10	Ricky Rudd	Tide Ford	159	Running	$73,450
21	34	75	Todd Bodine	Factory Stores of America Ford	159	Running	$66,300
22	29	26	Hut Stricklin	Quaker State Ford	159	Running	$61,700
23	38	23	Jimmy Spencer	Camel Cigarettes Ford	159	Running	$59,200
24	12	11	Brett Bodine	Lowe's Ford	159	Running	$67,700
25	32	42	Kyle Petty	Coors Light Pontiac	159	Running	$67,300
26	40	90	Mike Wallace	Heilig-Meyers Ford	158	Running	$55,975
27	6	87	Joe Nemechek	Burger King Chevrolet	158	Running	$51,675
28	21	33	Robert Pressley	Skoal Bandit Chevrolet	158	Running	$69,875
29	8	98	Jeremy Mayfield	RCA Ford	158	Running	$53,275
30	39	29	Steve Grissom	Meineke Chevrolet	158	Running	$52,675
31	28	41	Ricky Craven	Kodiak Chevrolet	158	Running	$52,675
32	35	22	Jimmy Hensley	MBNA America Pontiac	158	Running	$56,175
33	16	32	Greg Sacks	FINA/Lance Chevrolet	157	Running	$48,425
34	27	9	Lake Speed	Spam Ford	157	Running	$48,175
35	30	31	Ward Burton	Hardee's Chevrolet	154	Engine	$47,925
36	36	40	Rich Bickle	Kendall Pontiac	154	Running	$52,675
37	31	81	Kenny Wallace	T.I.C. Financial Systems Ford	152	Running	$47,625
38	18	8	Jeff Burton	Raybestos Ford	141	Running	$59,020
39	17	77	Bobby Hillin	Jasper Engines/USAir/Bryant H & C Ford	107	Engine	$47,920
40	37	12	Derrike Cope	Straight Arrow Ford	104	Engine	$52,520
41	41	27	Elton Sawyer	Hooters Ford	17	Valve Spring	$55,520
Total Posted Awards							**$4,447,015**

Legend: SP = Starting Position, FP = Finishing Position, # = Rookie • **Time of Race:** 2:34:37
Average Speed: 155.218 mph • **Margin of Victory:** 0.37 second • **Fastest Lap:** #3 Dale Earnhardt, Lap 131, 168.757 mph

Lap Leaders*

1–31	#24 Jeff Gordon	101–102	#25 Ken Schrader
32–33	#94 Bill Elliott	103–103	#30 Michael Waltrip
34–34	#37 John Andretti	104–104	#37 John Andretti
35–35	#77 Bobby Hillin	105–108	#24 Jeff Gordon
36–50	#4 Sterling Marlin	109–128	#2 Rusty Wallace
51–66	#94 Bill Elliott	129–129	#43 Bobby Hamilton
67–68	#18 Bobby Labonte	130–132	#37 John Andretti
69–69	#37 John Andretti	133–160	#3 Dale Earnhardt
70–71	#2 Rusty Wallace		
72–100	#94 Bill Elliott		

* 17 lead changes between 11 drivers
** Number of times in lead/number of laps led

Lap Leader Recap**

Bill Elliott	3/47
Jeff Gordon	2/35
Dale Earnhardt	1/28
Rusty Wallace	2/22
Sterling Marlin	1/15
John Andretti	4/6
Bobby Labonte	1/2
Ken Schrader	1/2
Bobby Hamilton	1/1
Bobby Hillin	1/1
Michael Waltrip	1/1

Caution Flags (1 for 4 laps)
133–136 J. Burton hit Turn 2 wall

21

BRICKYARD
400

INDIANAPOLIS MOTOR SPEEDWAY

AUGUST 3, 1996

JARRETT
Nips Irvan

A One-Two Punch for Robert Yates Racing

by Al Pearce

Before the 1996 race, it was almost universally accepted that it would take an extraordinary set of circumstances to win a Brickyard 400 from deep on the grid. Jeff Gordon won the 1994 race after starting 3rd, and Dale Earnhardt started 13th before winning the second annual race in 1995. The problem—at least everyone perceives it as a problem—is that the Indianapolis Motor Speedway offers few good opportunities for NASCAR stock cars to pass.

The 2.5-mile track is flat, rectangular, and unforgiving. It is especially treacherous when drivers are brazen enough (read as foolish enough) to venture very far outside the racing groove when either approaching or exiting any of the four distinctive corners. That "inside-at-all-costs" approach puts chasers at a disadvantage since drivers ahead of them have to merely protect the inside line. If anyone hopes to pass, he needs NASCAR's version of a stump-pulling motor, a sweet-handling car, just the right opportunity, and enough nerve and talent to put it all together.

That describes Dale Jarrett almost perfectly.

The second-generation driver won the 1996 Brickyard 400 and earned $564,035 for Robert Yates Racing with a late-race pass of

Ask no quarter and give none has always been a hallmark of NASCAR racing. The opening laps of the 1996 Brickyard were no exception as Ted Musgrave (PrimeStar Ford), Ricky Craven (Kodiak Chevrolet), Derrike Cope (Babcock Ford), Dale Jarrett (Quality Care Ford), and Joe Nemechek (Burger King Chevrolet) scrap for position.

BRICKYARD 400
AUGUST 3, 1996

great battle [with Jarrett], but we came up a little short. I washed up a little bit in Turn 1 and got in the marbles in Turn 2, then Dale got under me when I almost got in the fence. It was my race to win or lose, and I lost it. I think he would have had a real hard time passing me if I hadn't slipped. But I'm not going to make any excuses—I had the same race track as everybody else."

Jarrett's winning move came between Turns 1 and 2 on the 154th lap. He had been dogging Irvan for many laps, hoping against hope that his teammate might make a mistake and open the door ever so slightly. "Ernie went into Turn 1 kind of hard and couldn't get a good turn," Jarrett said of the race-winning pass. "My car turned good, so I went under him because I knew I might not get another chance. My car was a lot better once I got out in clean air. There might have been some oil on the track because I almost slid into Ernie, but I thought it was just because we were both so high."

Jarrett was using all the track and protecting his lead when a last-lap wreck involving Robert Pressley caused the race to end under caution. Jarrett started 24th—so much for qualifying up front—and led only twice on Laps 134–138 and then on the final seven. It was his third victory of the season (the previous two had been the Daytona 500 and Coca-Cola 600) and the seventh of his Winston Cup career. Behind Jarrett and Irvan in the top five were Terry Labonte, Mark Martin, and Morgan Shepherd.

The race started on a bad note when Darrell Waltrip blew up after just 9 of the 160 laps. All told, though, only 8 drivers would

After winning the 1994 race and the 1995 pole, Jeff Gordon's good fortunes at the Indianapolis Motor Speedway soured early in the 1996 Brickyard 400. Before he crashed, though, he'd started from the pole and led the first three laps.

stablemate Ernie Irvan. Combined, the two Ford Thunderbird drivers led six times for 50 laps and earned $831,320 for Yates' Charlotte, North Carolina-based team. It was Jarrett's second consecutive top-five finish at Indy (he crashed out in 1994) and Irvan's second late-race loss. (He suffered a flat tire while leading in the final moments of the inaugural race.)

"I'll tell you what," Irvan said after finishing second to Jarrett, "This is a lot more heartbreaking than that first one. This was a

Right
Front-row starters Jeff Gordon and Mark Martin lead the 40-car field to the green flag for the start of the 1996 race. Gordon crashed out and finished 37th; Martin led for 19 laps and finished a lead-lap 4th.

1996: Jarrett Nips Ervan

One of the most emotional moments of the third Brickyard 400 came early when 1995 winner Dale Earnhardt turned his Chevrolet Monte Carlo over to relief driver Mike Skinner. A week earlier, Earnhardt had suffered chest, shoulder, and collarbone injuries in a spectacular crash at Talladega.

The quick way around the Indianapolis Motor Speedway is on bottom, with left-side tires on the yellow line. After slipping just a bit, eventual second-place finisher Ernie Irvan finds himself hung on the outside, looking for an opening to get back in line.

Outside pole-sitter Mark Martin led once for 19 laps, finishing a lead-lap fourth. Here, the Roush Racing star leads third-place qualifier Lake Speed and pole-sitter Jeff Gordon during the opening 20 laps.

drop out of the 400—Waltrip, Ward Burton, and Ricky Craven with mechanical problems, and Kyle Petty, Sterling Marlin, Jeff Gordon, Kenny Wallace, and Robert Pressley after contact. Defending champion Dale Earnhardt started 12th but stayed in the Richard Childress-owned No. 3 Chevrolet for just 7 of the 160 laps. He was relieved by Mike Skinner, who drove the rest of the way and recorded a 15th-place for Earnhardt, who'd suffered a broken sternum and dislocated shoulder the weekend before in a crash at Talladega.

"I won't take a chance and do anything to injure myself or endanger anyone else," he said three days before the race. "My main focus right now is whether I can practice the car and run a lap good enough to make the field. I don't think it'll take much convincing to get me out of the car on Saturday. If I got in another crash it would put me even further behind in my career as far as this championship we're running for. We just want to hold our own this weekend and see how things go after it. Mike Skinner will do a good job if we can get him enough practice time this week. Once we get qualified, he'll be in the car more than I am."

Petty rode out the day's most spectacular accident, a four-banger that still ranks among the most unusual in NASCAR history. It began when he plowed into the Turn 4 wall after

Jeff Burton (No. 99 Ford), the newest member of the Roush Racing stable, can't keep Robert Yates Racing driver Ernie Irvan (No. 28 Ford) from passing on the inside during the 1996 race. Irvan finished 2nd, Burton 11th in the 160 lapper.

blowing a right-front tire at Lap 37. His Pontiac bounced off the wall and directly into the path of Sterling Marlin, who knocked Petty back into the wall. That lick (the third in the sequence) flung Petty back across the track, where he slammed the inside wall near the entrance to pit row. Other than being sore and dazed—and having a rescue worker accidentally step on his ponytail—Petty was no worse for the wear.

Four laps after Petty's crash, Jeff Gordon, the pole-sitter and 1994 race winner, crashed out after cutting down a tire in Turn 4. Kenny Wallace crashed out (but didn't bring out the caution) with just nine laps remaining, and Pressley caused the race to end under caution when he crashed in Turn 4 as Jarrett and the

rest of the front-runners came around for the checkered flag.

The first 21 starters finished on the lead lap, not surprising since the five caution periods were scattered in Laps 6 to 8, followed by 24 to 27, then 39 to 47 and 125 to 129, before the final caution at Lap 160. The 22nd through 28th finishers were one lap behind, with 29th-finishing Gary Bradberry two down. Pressley finished 157 laps before he crashed, and Bobby Hamilton, Greg Sacks, and Dave Marcis were the last three drivers still motoring around at the finish.

Jarrett's drive to the front was fairly uneventful. It took him only 20 laps to get from 24th on the grid to 15th. He briefly dropped to 24th again after a green-flag pit stop, then

Pole-sitter Jeff Gordon's impressive record at the Indianapolis Motor Speedway—1st in the first race, then 6th in the second—took a serious hit in the third. He was running 3rd when his No. 24 Chevrolet Monte Carlo crashed in Turn 4 on Lap 24. His crew got him back out for 16 more slow laps before Gordon finally gave up and took a 37th-place finish.

Ricky Rudd qualified poorly—he started only 35th—but drove a smart, consistent, error-free race to finish a lead-lap sixth in his self-owned No. 10 Ford Thunderbird.

26

started coming back to the front. "We knew we had a car capable of getting back through traffic," said rookie crew chief Todd Parrott. "It was just a matter of being careful at first and letting things settle down. Once we got toward the front, we knew we had a real shot at winning."

Jarrett reached the top 10 for the first time at Lap 60, dropped to 18th because of a pit stop almost halfway through the race, then reached 5th at Lap 100. Running 6th when the caution flag was waved for debris in Turn 1 at Lap 125, he took fuel only and came out 3rd behind Terry Labonte and Ricky Rudd. He passed Rudd to reach 2nd at Lap 132, then took the point from Labonte two laps later. But he was no match for Irvan, who powered by at Lap 139.

Irvan, back on the Winston Cup circuit after surviving a near-fatal crash at Michigan two years earlier, seemed unbeatable. "He was awfully strong," Jarrett said. "We're from the same team, so I know his car and his engine are as good as mine. I really didn't know if I could pass him in the final laps. He was running a good line, the same line he'd been running all afternoon. It was the line I wanted, but I knew he wasn't going to give it up without a hard fight. When my chance came, I went for it because I knew I might not get another one."

In all fairness, Irvan might have been a victim of oil or water on the track. Moments after smoke began billowing from the back of Kenny Wallace's slowing car, Irvan entered Turn 1 just as he had the previous 152 laps. But his

A couple of NASCAR's brightest young stars raced hard in the 1996 Brickyard 400. Jeff Burton (No. 99 Roush Racing Ford) finished a lead-lap 11th, while Jeremy Mayfield (No. 98 Yarborough Racing Ford) was a lap-down 25th.

Leader Ernie Irvan works hard to overtake the No. 41 Chevrolet of Ricky Craven in the final laps of the 1996 race. Moments later, Irvan slipped high in Turn 1, and Robert Yates Racing teammate Dale Jarrett (No. 88 Ford) slipped by and drove away to a 1-second victory.

Ford lost purchase for an instant and slipped nearly 6 feet up the track. Just far enough behind to avoid a similar fate, Jarrett cranked his steering wheel to the left, pulled to the inside, and made the winning pass.

"When Ernie's car took off up the track, I wondered what had happened," Jarrett said. "I felt a little something down there [on the track in Turns 1 and 2], but it didn't bother me like it obviously bothered Ernie. I don't know if it was oil or water, but something made him slip up the track like that. It's unfortunate for him, but that's the way racing sometimes is."

Surprisingly, Jarrett wasn't the only strong finisher to come from deep on the grid. Shepherd started 38th and finished 5th, and Rudd started 35th and finished 6th. Rusty Wallace came from 17th to 7th, and Rookie of the Year candidate Johnny Benson Jr. led three times for 70 laps and came from 14th on the grid to finish 8th.

So much for conventional wisdom about track position and winning from the front.

Winner Dale Jarrett and his wife, Kelli, celebrate their $564,035 victory in the 1996 Brickyard 400. Jarrett started 24th and led laps 135–138 then passed his teammate, Ernie Irvan, with just 7 laps remaining in the 160-lap race.

OFFICIAL BOX SCORE

Third Brickyard 400–August 3, 1996
Indianapolis Motor Speedway • NASCAR Winston Cup Series

FP	SP	Car	Driver	Car Name & Brand	Laps Comp	Running/ Reason	Prize Money
1	24	88	Dale Jarrett	Quality Care/Ford Credit Ford	160	139.508	$564,035
2	15	28	Ernie Irvan	Texaco Havoline Ford	160	Running	$267,285
3	9	5	Terry Labonte	Kellogg's Corn Flakes Chevrolet	160	Running	$209,535
4	2	6	Mark Martin	Valvoline Ford	160	Running	$195,235
5	38	75	Morgan Shepherd	Remington Arms Ford	160	Running	$140,135
6	35	10	Ricky Rudd	Tide Ford	160	Running	$118,385
7	17	2	Rusty Wallace	Miller Ford	160	Running	$112,985
8	14	30	Johnny Benson Jr.	Pennzoil Pontiac	160	Running	$166,485
9	8	1	Rick Mast	Hooters Pontiac	160	Running	$99,485
10	7	94	Bill Elliott	McDonald's Ford	160	Running	$98,585
11	28	99	Jeff Burton	Exide Batteries Ford	160	Running	$82,260
12	20	23	Jimmy Spencer	Camel Cigarettes Ford	160	Running	$87,660
13	3	9	Lake Speed	Spam Ford	160	Running	$82,360
14	36	12	Derrike Cope	Badcock Ford	160	Running	$77,960
15	12	3	Dale Earnhardt	GM Goodwrench Service Chevrolet	160	Running	$84,460
16	4	25	Ken Schrader	Budweiser Chevrolet	160	Running	$77,440
17	18	15	Wally Dallenbach Jr.	Hayes Modems Ford	160	Running	$74,660
18	16	8	Hut Stricklin	Circuit City Ford	160	Running	$66,560
19	27	37	John Andretti	Kmart/Little Caesars Ford	160	Running	$72,460
20	29	7	Geoff Bodine	QVC Ford	160	Running	$73,160
21	21	16	Ted Musgrave	Family Channel/PRIMESTAR Ford	160	Running	$70,260
22	22	11	Brett Bodine	Lowe's Ford	159	Running	$69,160
23	25	90	Dick Trickle	Heilig-Meyers Ford	159	Running	$61,060
24	23	18	Bobby Labonte	Interstate Batteries Chevrolet	159	Running	$72,960
25	19	98	Jeremy Mayfield	RCA Ford	159	Running	$59,160
26	5	77	Bobby Hillin Jr.	Jasper Engines Ford	159	Running	$54,935
27	6	87	Joe Nemechek	Burger King Chevrolet	159	Running	$63,935
28	30	21	Michael Waltrip	Citgo Ford	159	Running	$62,435
29	26	95	Gary Bradberry	Shoney's Restaurant Ford	158	Running	$54,935
30	34	33	Robert Pressley	Skoal Bandit Chevrolet	157	Accident	$58,935
31	37	43	Bobby Hamilton	STP Pontiac	156	Running	$58,435
32	10	29	Greg Sacks	Cartoon Network Chevrolet	154	Running	$57,935
33	31	81	Kenny Wallace	Square D/TIC Ford	151	Engine	$50,865
34	39	41	Ricky Craven	Kodiak Chevrolet Pinion	142	Broken	$57,435
35	40	71	Dave Marcis	Prodigy Chevrolet	112	Running	$50,185
36	32	22	Ward Burton	MBNA America Pontiac	82	Engine	$64,935
37	1	24	Jeff Gordon	DuPont Refinishes Chevrolet	40	Accident	$137,591
38	13	42	Kyle Petty	Coors Light Pontiac	37	Accident	$56,780
39	11	4	Sterling Marlin	Kodak Film Chevrolet	37	Accident	$67,380
40	33	17	Darrell Waltrip	Parts America Chevrolet	9	Engine	$56,780

Total Posted Awards

$4,695,547
(plus $150,000
in merchandise)

Legend: SP = Starting Position, FP = Finishing Position, # = Rookie • **Time of Race:** 2:52:02 • **Average Speed:** 139.508 mph
Margin of Victory: 0.936 second (under yellow • **Fastest Lap:** #28 Ernie Irvan, Lap 133, 171.340 mph
Fastest Leading Lap: #6 Mark Martin, Lap 12, 170.934 mph

Lap Leaders*

1–3	#24 Jeff Gordon	117–120	#30 Johnny Benson Jr.
4–22	#6 Mark Martin	121–121	#10 Ricky Rudd
23–24	#9 Lake Speed	122–126	#28 Ernie Irvan
25–25	#3 Dale Earnhardt	127–134	#5 Terry Labonte
26–27	#25 Ken Schrader	135–138	#88 Dale Jarrett
28–28	#4 Sterling Marlin	139–153	#28 Ernie Irvan
29–30	#94 Bill Elliott	154–160	#88 Dale Jarrett
31–31	#42 Kyle Petty		
32–72	#30 Johnny Benson Jr.		
73–82	#28 Ernie Irvan		
83–107	#30 Johnny Benson Jr.	* 18 lead changes between 13 drivers	
108–116	#28 Ernie Irvan	** Number of times in lead/number of laps led	

Lap Leader Recap**

J. Benson Jr.	3/70
Ernie Irvan	4/39
Mark Martin	1/19
Dale Jarrett	2/11
Terry Labonte	1/8
Jeff Gordon	1/3
Ken Schrader	1/2
Bill Elliott	1/2
Lake Speed	1/2
Dale Earnhardt	1/1
Sterling Marlin	1/1
Kyle Petty	1/1
Ricky Rudd	1/1

Caution Flags (5 for 21 laps)

6–8	Spin Turn 2: #41, 71, 77, 33
24–27	Accident Turn 4: #24
39–47	Accident Turn 4: #42, 4
126–129	Debris on track: #43
160–160	Accident Turn 4: #33

RUDD'S
Gamble Pays Off

Late Caution Flag Lets Rudd Outlast Labonte

by Al Pearce

Somebody should have seen this one coming. Nobody seemed to notice that steady and consistent Ricky Rudd had been a quiet yet unmistakable force in two of the first three Brickyard 400s. By the time he and his No. 10 Rudd Performance Motorsports Ford Thunderbird arrived for the August 2, 1997, race, they knew what it would take to win NASCAR's second most-important event.

Rudd had already won a 500-miler at Dover in June. That victory extended his career winning streak to 15 consecutive years and thus relieved him of the inevitable outside pressure to keep the streak alive. Even so, he came into the fourth annual stock car race at the Indianapolis Motor Speedway on something of an inconsistent roller coaster. He had placed 1st, 21st, 13th, 3rd, 34th, 9th, and 36th in his previous seven starts of 1997. The Brickyard 400 stopped the ride with a dramatic late-race victory that was unquestionably the biggest of his career.

Rudd qualified seventh, then maintained a low-profile, error-free, consistent pace all afternoon. He was lower than eighth only once when he made a 20-second stop for gas and four fresh tires under the green flag at Lap 40.

After completing all but one lap of the first three Brickyard 400s (lead-lap 11th in the inaugural race, one-down 20th in the second, and a solid lead-lap 6th in the third). Ricky Rudd and his No. 10 Tide Ford had shown they knew their way around the Indianapolis Motor Speedway. Here, the 1997 race winner passes fellow Ford driver Michael Waltrip on the victory lap.

BRICKYARD 400
AUGUST 2, 1997

Ernie Irvan's pole-winning No. 28 Havoline Ford and the No. 40 BellSouth Chevrolet of Joe Nemechek started the 1996 Brickyard 400 from the front row. Both were running at the finish, Irvan a lead-lap 10th and Nemechek a lap down in 32nd.

Ernie Irvan's crew pushes their Robert Yates Racing No. 28 Havoline Ford back to the garage after a pre-race practice session. Irvan finished a lead-lap 10th, his second top 10 in his three Brickyard 400 appearances.

He spent the second half of the race among the top five, taking the lead for the first time at Lap 114 by stretching his Tide-sponsored car's fuel during an exchange of pit stops under caution.

Mike Skinner (Laps 115–122), Jeff Gordon (123–135), and Dale Jarrett (136–146) swapped the lead down the stretch, each looking at times like they might win the race. All the while, Rudd was following in their wake, running as lightly as he could and saving fuel for what he and crew chief Jim Long realized would be an economy run to the checkered flag. When a debris caution waved at Lap 147, the front five runners pitted for fresh tires and a splash of gas to prepare for an all-out run to the finish. This left Rudd, Bobby Labonte, Johnny Benson Jr., Ricky Craven, and Mark Martin in the top five for the restart at Lap 151. Any fuel concerns Rudd might have had faded when Rich Bickle crashed at Lap 153, thus slowing the pace (and saving fuel) for three laps. "I wanted to go ahead and get the race over with," Rudd said later, "but the more caution laps we ran, the better our fuel mileage looked. It was going to be tight if we'd

Virginia native Ricky Rudd came into the fifth annual Brickyard 400 on a streak of having won at least one NASCAR Winston Cup race every season for 16 consecutive years.

Below
Bobby Labonte (No. 18 Interstate Pontiac), Dale Earnhardt (No. 3 Goodwrench Chevrolet), and Ted Musgrave (No. 16 Family Channel Ford) finished 2nd, 29th, and 33rd, respectively, in the fourth annual Brickyard 400.

Third-place starter (he finished in that same position) and 1996 race winner Dale Jarrett takes four tires and gas during one of his five pit stops. He stopped twice under green-flag conditions and four times during cautions, including a gas-only stop with just 13 laps remaining.

gone green all the way, so the cautions really played into our hands."

The last green-flag dash was for three laps. With all the pressure in the world on his shoulders, Rudd restarted smoothly and beat Bobby Labonte by .183 seconds, the closest margin of victory in any Brickyard 400 race so far. Defending champion Jarrett was a fast-closing third, 1994 champion Gordon was fourth, and, somewhat-surprisingly, Jeremy Mayfield was fifth.

The rest of the top-10 finishers were Mark Martin, Johnny Benson Jr., Bill Elliott, rookie Mike Skinner, and Ernie Irvan, the race's top lap-leader. The top-10 finishers shared in the race's $5-million purse. It was another frustrating day for Irvan, who had fallen from 1st to 17th with a flat tire in the final laps of the 1994 race. After missing the 1995 race due to serious injuries suffered in August 1994, he lost the 1996 race when teammate Dale Jarrett passed him in the final laps.

A record 23 of the 43 starters were on the lead lap after 160 laps, 5 others were only one lap down, and another 7 were more laps

behind but running at the finish. Among the notables that did not finish—Sterling Marlin with engine problems after just two laps and Terry Labonte, Rusty Wallace, Wally Dallenbach Jr., and David Green, all with engine problems. Jeff Purvis finished 48 laps behind after having his car's radiator replaced, and accidents slowed the pace of Michael Waltrip, Chad Little, Derrike Cope, and Rich Bickle.

Bobby Labonte said his car was good but not fast enough, so he was thrilled to finish perhaps 15 positions better than he thought he would. "We had good track position, and that's what it's all about here," he said. "We were at the right place at the right time, and that was behind Ricky on the last restart. All day, the race came to us because the cautions were at the right time. We had good luck on our side, and we knew we'd rather finish second than screw up and finish worse."

Kyle Petty started 39th and finished a lead-lap 13th in his new No. 44 Hot Wheels Pontiac. After several years with flamboyant team owner Felix Sabates, the third-generation NASCAR racer formed his own team in co-ownership with his father, Richard Petty.

It was a bittersweet week for Winston Cup Rookie of the Year candidate Mike Skinner. He destroyed his primary car in a pre-qualifying practice crash, then qualified sixth and finished a lead-lap ninth in his No. 31 Lowe's Chevrolet backup car from Richard Childress Racing.

Rudd made no apologies for winning the way he did. "We weren't the fastest car, but it's not like we backed into it either," he said. "We were up front and among the leaders all afternoon. Every race team goes into a race with a strategy or a game plan, and they usually change during the race. When we realized how good our gas mileage was, we began to make that part of our strategy. We didn't stop when everyone else did because track position is so important and our tire wear was still good. For a change, things worked right into our hands with the late cautions."

As Rudd well knows, getting there first is all that matters.

Wisconsin native Johnny Benson Jr. backed up his eighth-place finish in the 1996 race (he led that one three times for 70 laps) with a lead-lap seventh-place finish in the 1997 Brickyard 400.

Mark Martin made an impressive charge from 31st on the grid to a lead-lap finish of 6th. After finishing 35th in the inaugural Brickyard 400, the Arkansas native was a lead-lap 5th, 4th, and 6th in the next three races.

Right
The only multi-car accident during the 1997 race came early, when Derrike Cope (No. 36 Skittles Pontiac), Michael Waltrip (No. 21 Citgo Ford), Ted Musgrave (No. 16 Family Channel Ford), and Bill Elliott (No. 94 McDonald's Ford) spun together in Turn 2 at Lap 15. Cope was sidelined on the spot, and Waltrip lost many laps in the pits for repairs.

Left
The potent Hendrick Motorsports organization had three Chevrolet Monte Carlos in the 1996 Brickyard, including the No. 25 Budweiser-sponsored car that took Ricky Craven to a 16th-place finish.

Below
Battling midway through the 1997 race are Darrell Waltrip (No. 17 Western Auto Chevrolet), Jeremy Mayfield (No. 37 K-Mart Ford), 1994 race-winner Jeff Gordon (No. 24 DuPont Chevrolet), Kenny Wallace (No. 81 Square-D Ford), and 1997 winner Ricky Rudd (No. 10 Tide Ford).

Ricky Rudd squeezed every ounce of fuel from his No. 10 Tide Ford in winning the 1997 Brickyard 400. He ran the entire 160 laps with only one change of left-side tires and didn't make another pit stop after taking four tires and gas under caution at Lap 114. Two late-race cautions that slowed the pace allowed Rudd to conserve just enough fuel to finish several car-lengths ahead of Bobby Labonte.

OFFICIAL BOX SCORE

Fourth Brickyard 400–August 2, 1997
Indianapolis Motor Speedway • NASCAR Winston Cup Series

SP	FP	Car	Driver	Car Name & Brand	Laps Comp	Running/ Reason	Prize Money
1	7	10	Ricky Rudd	Tide Ford	160	130.828	$571,000
2	25	18	Bobby Labonte	Interstate Batteries Pontiac	160	Running	$242,275
3	3	88	Dale Jarrett	Quality Care/Ford Credit Ford	160	Running	$223,900
4	24	24	Jeff Gordon	DuPont Refinishes Chevrolet	160	Running	$223,675
5	16	37	Jeremy Mayfield	Kmart/RC Cola Ford	160	Running	$142,445
6	31	6	Mark Martin	Valvoline Ford	160	Running	$125,960
7	20	30	Johnny Benson Jr.	Pennzoil Pontiac	160	Running	$121,760
8	15	94	Bill Elliott	McDonald's Ford	160	Running	$110,460
9	6	31	#Mike Skinner	Lowe's Chevrolet	160	Running	$132,560
10	1	28	Ernie Irvan	Texaco Havoline Ford	160	Running	$143,560
11	8	33	Ken Schrader	Skoal Chevrolet	160	Running	$95,235
12	27	9	Lake Speed	Melling Engine Parts Ford	160	Running	$83,135
13	39	44	Kyle Petty	Hot Wheels Pontiac	160	Running	$78,035
14	4	17	Darrell Waltrip	Parts America Chevrolet	160	Running	$85,085
15	33	99	Jeff Burton	Exide Batteries Ford	160	Running	$96,885
16	41	25	Ricky Craven	Budweiser Chevrolet	160	Running	$82,135
17	35	98	John Andretti	RCA Ford	160	Running	$80,095
18	42	11	Brett Bodine	Close Call Ford	160	Running	$79,535
19	36	22	Ward Burton	MBNA America Pontiac	160	Running	$78,435
20	12	43	Bobby Hamilton	STP Pontiac	160	Running	$82,935
21	34	27	Rick Wilson	Indianapolis Colts Ford	160	Running	$65,935
22	23	92	Ron Barfield Jr.	New Holland Ford	160	Running	$64,935
23	17	75	Rick Mast	Remington Arms Ford	160	Running	$74,335
24	40	23	Jimmy Spencer	Camel Ford	159	Running	$74,435
25	26	29	#Jeff Green	Cartoon Network Chevrolet	159	Running	$67,735
26	19	41	Steve Grissom	Kodiak Chevrolet	159	Running	$71,010
27	30	95	Ed Berrier	Realtree Chevrolet	159	Running	$59,910
28	11	40	Robby Gordon	Coors Light Chevrolet	159	Running	$68,910
29	5	3	Dale Earnhardt	GM Goodwrench Service Plus Chevrolet	158	Running	$76,310
30	29	81	Kenny Wallace	Square D Ford	158	Running	$67,910
31	37	91	Greg Sacks	Kruse International Chevrolet	158	Running	$57,410
32	2	42	Joe Nemechek	BellSouth Chevrolet	156	Running	$67,910
33	22	16	Ted Musgrave	Family Channel/ Primestar Ford	155	Running	$63,660
34	10	26	Rich Bickle	KFC Team Twister Chevrolet	153	Accident	$56,410
35	9	96	#David Green	Caterpillar Chevrolet	137	Engine	$56,160
36	14	46	Wally Dallenbach Jr.	First Union Chevrolet	120	Ignition	$61,510
37	28	12	Jeff Purvis	Gazelle/QVC Chevrolet	112	Running	$55,876
38	43	2	Rusty Wallace	Miller Lite Ford	91	Engine	$72,755
39	18	21	Michael Waltrip	Citgo Ford	89	Running	$62,755
40	38	5	Terry Labonte	Kellogg's Chevrolet	83	Engine	$77,755
41	32	36	Derrike Cope	Skittles Pontiac	12	Accident	$55,755
42	21	97	Chad Little	John Deere Pontiac	2	Accident	$55,755
43	13	4	Sterling Marlin	Kodak Film Chevrolet	2	Engine	$71,755

TOTAL POSTED AWARDS $4,965,217

Legend: SP = Starting Position, FP = Finishing Position, # = Rookie

Time of Race: 3:03:26:841 • **Average Speed**: 130.828 mph • **Margin of Victory**: 0.183 second

Lap Leaders*
1–39	#28 Ernie Irvan
40–40	#24 Jeff Gordon
41–41	#30 Johnny Benson Jr.
42–54	#46 Wally Dallenbach Jr.
55–55	#23 Jimmy Spencer
56–56	#5 Terry Labonte
57–57	#25 Ricky Craven
58–77	#88 Dale Jarrett
78–80	#24 Jeff Gordon
81–81	#30 Johnny Benson Jr.
82–83	#23 Jimmy Spencer

Lap Leaders* (cont.)
85–88	#24 Jeff Gordon
89–109	#99 Jeff Burton
110–113	#24 Jeff Gordon
114–114	#10 Ricky Rudd
115–122	#31 Mike Skinner
123–135	#24 Jeff Gordon
136–146	#88 Dale Jarrett
147–160	#10 Ricky Rudd
* 19 changes between 11 drivers	
** Number of times in lead/number of laps led	

Lap Leader Recap**
Ernie Irvan	1/39
Dale Jarrett	2/31
Jeff Gordon	5/25
Jeff Burton	1/21
Ricky Rudd	2/15
W. Dallenbach Jr.	2/14
Mike Skinner	1/8
Jimmy Spencer	2/3
J. Benson Jr.	2/2
Ricky Craven	1/1
Terry Labonte	1/184–84

Caution Flags (6 for 25 laps)
4–6
15–20
84–88
114–117
147–150
155–157

#46 Wally Dallenbach Jr.

GORDON
Cleans Up

The Rainbow Warrior Repeats

by Al Pearce

Nobody knew it at the time, but the outcome of the fifth annual Brickyard 400 was almost certainly decided by the halfway point. It would take the final 80 laps for number three starter Jeff Gordon to become the first two-time winner of NASCAR's second-biggest race. But it was an uneventful ride he gladly endured in exchange for the $1.6 million waiting in Victory Lane.

There were moments during the first half of the 160-lap race when outside pole-sitter Dale Jarrett seemed a cinch for his second Indianapolis Motor Speedway victory. His Robert Yates-owned/Todd Parrott-prepared Ford Taurus appeared to be the only car capable of keeping up with hometown hero and pre-race favorite Gordon in his Chevrolet Monte Carlo. "Dale had the only car I saw all afternoon that was able to pass other good cars and drive away from them," Gordon said. "He was the one I was most worried about."

But Jarrett's bid fizzled when he ran out of gas entering Turn 1 early in the 81st lap. With Indy's four flat turns, two short straightaways, and two long straights, there was no chance he could coast around to the pits and stay on the lead lap. In fact, he lost two laps during his silent glide back to pit road in Turn 4. Even

A familiar sight at the Indianapolis Motor Speedway: Jeff Gordon leading the field. In pursuit of the two-time winner at the 1998 Brickyard 400 are Jeremy Mayfield and Dale Jarrett.

BRICKYARD 400
AUGUST 1, 1998

Jeff Gordon (right) and Ward Burton talk things over just before the 1998 Brickyard 400. Gordon started 3rd and finished 1st; Burton started 30th and finished 34th.

then, he lost two more laps as crew members from both his team and that of Robert Yates Racing teammate Kenny Irwin sprinted to the car and pushed it the length of pit road before finally changing its tires and refilling its 22-gallon fuel tank.

With his primary rival suddenly out of contention, Gordon had things his own way the rest of the afternoon. He took the lead for good at Lap 127 and easily beat Mark Martin, Bobby Labonte, Mike Skinner, and Dale Earnhardt. The next five positions in the $5 million-plus race were held by pole-sitter Ernie Irvan, John Andretti, Rusty Wallace, Terry Labonte, and Ken Schrader. As for Jarrett—he used several perfectly-timed caution periods to make up his four-lap deficit, charging from 30th to 16th in the final laps.

Not surprisingly, Jarrett, the 1996 Brickyard 400 winner and 1997 Winston Cup points

Ernie Irvan qualified No. 1 for the 1998 Brickyard 400, the second pole in his four Indianapolis Motor Speedway appearances. He also started No. 1 for the Robert Yates-owned team in 1997.

runner-up was none too happy. "We had a great race car, a super race car, in fact, but we ran out of gas," he said curtly. "I drive the race car, and I come in when they tell me to come in. That's all I do. We ran out of gas. Now, what else do you want to know?"

Todd Parrott wasn't willing to offer any further insight, but his brother, team member Brad, did. "We thought we could get through Lap 81 but were a lap short," he said. "Evidently, we didn't think we'd burn as much gas as we did outrunning them and building a 2 1/2-second lead. We talked to Dale about trying to save a little fuel, but this is a big track, and it bit us. It was bad fate, and hopefully it won't happen again."

Jarrett was leading—indeed, he had led 26 consecutive laps and was pulling away—when he ran out of gas. Gordon had led Laps 19–38 and 46–53, then led twice more for 69 of the

NASCAR president Bill France, Jr. gave the 43 drivers the command to start their engines for the 1998 Brickyard 400. It was the first time in quite some time that a member of the Hulman or George families had not started a race at the Indianapolis Motor Speedway.

Jeff Gordon and the No. 24 Hendrick Motorsports Chevrolet Monte Carlo won the inaugural Brickyard 400 in 1994 and the fifth annual race in 1998.

Nineteen ninety-four and 1998 winner Jeff Gordon (No. 24 Chevrolet) battles 1996 winner Dale Jarrett in the early stages of the 1998 Brickyard 400. Jarrett was a contender to win until running out of gas near the midpoint of the 160-lap race.

Right
The Brickyard 400 is the best-attended race on the Winston Cup schedule.

The Todd Parrott-led crew give Dale Jarrett right-side tires and another tank of gas during the 1998 Brickyard 400. After a fuel miscalculation put him four laps behind at the halfway point, Jarrett fought back to a lead-lap 16th-place finish.

Upper right
Bobby Labonte has been tantalizingly close to Victory Lane twice in the Brickyard 400. He was second to winner Ricky Rudd in the 1997 race and third behind Jeff Gordon and Mark Martin in 1998.

Right
Mike Skinner didn't get credit for his Brickyard 400 debut in 1996 as he relief drove most of the race for the injured Dale Earnhardt. But he got plenty of credit in 1997 when he started 6th and finished 9th—and in 1998 when he started 16th and finished 4th for team owner Richard Childress.

final 76 laps. Other lap-leaders included Ernie Irvan, Dale Earnhardt, Terry Labonte, Mark Martin, and Robert Pressley, although none of them posed a serious threat to Gordon.

Or did they? Crew chief Ray Evernham didn't get many takers when he tried to convince the press corps that both Jarrett and Jeremy Mayfield (who crashed out early) were in position to win the race. "I'm telling you," he said emphatically during the winner's interview, "We were flat lucky today. We didn't win it as much as two faster Fords lost it. When the 88 [of Jarrett] and the 12 [of Mayfield] had their problems, then the 6 [of Martin] was really the car we had to race.

But I don't think we ever thought we had it safely in-hand. We never thought it was going to be easy."

However, Gordon's ability to lead and stay in "clean air" was an enormous advantage. Aerodynamics are key on a flat and fast track like Indy, so engineers work tirelessly to plant their cars' noses on the pavement. And the trick to that, Gordon said, is to lead. "The hardest thing about this track is trying to pull out and pass somebody," he said. "The only strategy Ray and I had was to stay out front as long as we could, to make other people come after us. Every time I got right up behind another car to pass, the nose started pushing

Jeremy Mayfield and the Mobil 1 team's Brickyard outing was disappointing, but his season was stellar. He and fellow Penske driver Rusty Wallace consistently ran up front in 1998. With Penske's strong cars and veteran crew chief Paul Andrews at the helm, Mayfield has become a force to watch in Winston Cup competition.

Below
Indianapolis native and Winston Cup rookie Kenny Irwin had a solid top-10 run going until crashing the Robert Yates-owned No. 28 Ford Taurus in the 1998 Brickyard 400. After starting a stunning 4th, he finished a disappointing 38th.

The Jimmy Fennig-led crew prepares to service the No. 6 Ford Taurus of Mark Martin moments after Jeff Gordon leaves the pits during the 1998 Brickyard 400.

Left
After missing 15 races because of injuries received in March, rookie Steve Park made his return at the 1998 Brickyard 400. He started his Chevrolet Monte Carlo 25th and finished 35th, the victim of a late-race cut tire that caused him to wreck with just 12 laps remaining.

Far left
Ford Taurus driver Mark Martin leads fellow Taurus loyalist Brett Bodine and Pontiac driver Kyle Petty during the 1998 Brickyard 400. Martin finished 2nd, Bodine 33rd, and Petty a lead-lap 14th.

[refusing to turn]. That's why I wanted to get out front and stay out there."

Typically, Gordon tried to downplay his role in the victory. He praised Evernham for preparing a car every bit as good as the 1994-winning Chevrolet. He spoke of God's help (as he often does), then came down to the bottom line of this Brickyard 400. "When it's your day, it's your day," he said. "Everything we did was like clockwork, and nothing went wrong. And it seemed like something happened to all the other guys we were having to race. This just blows me away."

Others weren't so fortunate. Ricky Rudd, Steve Park, and Jimmy Spencer crashed late and missed out on good finishes. Rusty Wallace had a flat tire and ran out of gas but still managed to finish eighth. Ward Burton ran out of gas and sat idle on the Turn 3 apron for several laps before NASCAR finally waved the caution. Mayfield was strong until he crashed, and Pressley, Chad Little, and Jeff Green were involved in a late crash that caused the race to end under caution. Early contender Jeff Burton lost many laps with drivetrain problems,

Sterling Marlin (No. 40 Chevrolet) and Rusty Wallace battle during the 1998 Brickyard 400. Marlin started 11th and finished in that same position; Wallace started 14th and finished 8th.

This late-race, multi-car accident on a restart caused the 1998 Brickyard 400 to end under caution. It damaged several cars and eliminated on the spot defending champion Ricky Rudd.

Above right
Quick service from the Tony Furr-led team helped Rick Craven finish a credible 17th in the 1998 Brickyard 400. It was Craven's third start since post-concussion syndrome convinced him to take himself out of the No. 50 Budweiser-sponsored, Hendrick Motorsports-owned Chevrolet Monte Carlo.

but they were solved back in the garage area and he came out running at the finish.

The 2nd-place finish was especially bitter for Mark Martin, whose first four Brickyard 400s had seen him finish 35th, 5th, 4th, and 6th. "We're doing all we can do," he said, "but things just haven't gone our way up here. This is the same car that won earlier this year at Las Vegas, Texas, and California, so we know it's good enough. But that 24 car [of Gordon] is just too good right now. We thought we had some horsepower to run with him, but, man, he just flew down the straightaways."

And Gordon wasn't too shabby making the last left-hander either—the turn into Victory Lane.

Jeff Gordon, winner of the inaugural Brickyard 400 in 1994, became the event's only two-time winner in 1998. His most recent victory was worth a $1 million bonus from the R. J. Reynolds Tobacco Co. as part of its No Bull 5 program.

Left
Jeremy Mayfield started 12th and was running near the front when he lost control and crashed in Turn 2 during the 1998 Brickyard 400. His Kranefuss-Penske No. 12 Ford Taurus eventually made it back on the track, but it finally retired after 67 laps with handling problems.

OFFICIAL BOX SCORE

Fifth Brickyard 400–August 1, 1998

Indianapolis Motor Speedway • NASCAR Winston Cup Series

FP	SP	Car	Driver	Car Name & Brand	Laps Comp	Running/ Reason	Prize Money
1	3	24	Jeff Gordon	DuPont Chevrolet	160	126.770	$1,637,625
2	7	6	Mark Martin	Valvoline Ford	160	Running	$248,375
3	10	18	Bobby Labonte	Interstate Batteries Pontiac	160	Running	$224,525
4	16	31	Mike Skinner	Lowe's Chevrolet	160	Running	$187,325
5	28	3	Dale Earnhardt	GM Goodwrench Chevrolet	160	Running	$169,275
6	1	36	Ernie Irvan	Skittles Pontiac	160	Running	$159,260
7	9	43	John Andretti	STP Pontiac	160	Running	$138,160
8	14	2	Rusty Wallace	Miller Lite Ford	160	Running	$126,360
9	8	5	Terry Labonte	Kellogg's et al Chevrolet	160	Running	$133,135
10	19	33	Ken Schrader	Skoal Chevrolet	160	Running	$119,835
11	11	40	Sterling Marlin	Coors Light Chevrolet	160	Running	$100,760
12	37	94	Bill Elliott	McDonald's Ford	160	Running	$102,110
13	43	35	Darrell Waltrip	Tabasco Pepper Sauce Chevrolet	160	Running	$89,610
14	33	44	Kyle Petty	Hot Wheels Pontiac	160	Running	$96,010
15	36	91	Morgan Shepherd	Little Joe's Autos Chevrolet	160	Running	$91,810
16	2	88	Dale Jarrett	Quality Care/Ford Credit Ford	160	Running	$140,260
17	6	50	Ricky Craven	Budweiser Chevrolet	160	Running	$92,810
18	18	90	Dick Trickle	Heilig-Meyers/Simmons Ford	160	Running	$91,610
19	38	16	Ted Musgrave	Primestar Ford	160	Running	$90,910
20	24	4	Bobby Hamilton	Kodak Film Chevrolet	160	Running	$95,960
21	29	21	Michael Waltrip	CITGO Petroleum Ford	160	Running	$93,410
22	42	75	Rick Mast	Remington Arms Ford	160	Running	$81,310
23	26	41	Steve Grissom	Kodiak Chevrolet	160	Running	$86,210
24	17	42	Joe Nemechek	BellSouth Chevrolet	160	Running	$85,110
25	39	26	Johnny Benson Jr.	Cheerios Ford	159	Running	$84,310
26	41	9	Jerry Nadeau	Cartoon Network/Melling Ford	159	Running	$81,885
27	15	00	Buckshot Jones	Real Tree Extra Chevrolet	158	Running	$72,285
28	35	97	Chad Little	John Deere Ford	157	Accident	$73,985
29	20	77	Robert Pressley	Jasper Engines & Trans Ford	157	Accident	$84,085
30	5	46	Jeff Green	The Money Store Chevrolet	157	Running	$69,785
31	27	10	Ricky Rudd	Tide/Whirlpool Ford	155	Accident	$85,685
32	21	23	Jimmy Spencer	Winston Cigarettes Ford	154	Accident	$78,285
33	40	11	Brett Bodine	Paychex Ford	152	Running	$75,535
34	30	22	Ward Burton	MBNA America Pontiac	151	Running	$75,285
35	25	1	Steve Park	Pennzoil Chevrolet	148	Accident	$68,025
36	34	99	Jeff Burton	Exide Batteries Ford	145	Running	$84,385
37	13	7	Geoff Bodine	Philips Communications Ford	124	Vibration	$74,745
38	4	28	Kenny Irwin Jr.	Texaco/Havoline Ford	116	Accident	$98,805
39	31	98	Rich Bickle	Thorn Apple Valley Ford	112	Running	$74,650
40	22	13	Wally Dallenbach Jr.	First Plus Financial Ford	102	Engine	$67,645
41	32	71	Dave Marcis	Realtree Chevrolet	102	Engine	$67,635
42	12	12	Jeremy Mayfield	Mobil 1 Ford	67	Handling	$74,630
43	23	81	Kenny Wallace	Square D Ford	65	Engine	$67,630

TOTAL POSTED AWARDS $5,941,040

Time of Race: 3:09:19.165 • Average Speed: 126.770 mph • Margin of Victory: Under Caution
Fastest Leading Lap: #24 Jeff Gordon, Lap 109 - 172.180 mph

Lap Leaders

1–18	Ernie Irvan #36
19–38	Jeff Gordon #24
39–45	Ernie Irvan #36
46–53	Jeff Gordon #24
54–80	Dale Jarrett #88
81–81	Mark Martin #6
82–83	Terry Labonte #5
84–118	Jeff Gordon #24
119–120	Robert Pressley #77
121–126	Dale Earnhardt #3
127–160	Jeff Gordon #24

Lap Leader Recap

Jeff Gordon	97
Dale Jarrett	27
Ernie Irvan	25
Dale Earnhardt	6
Terry Labonte	2
Robert Pressley	2
Mark Martin	2

Caution Flags (9 for 34 laps)

18–22	Accident Turn 1: #7
36–40	Accident Turn 2: #12
87–90	#22 Stalled Turn 3
95–98	Accident Turn 4: #00, #11
104–107	Oil Turn 3: #13
118–122	Spin Turn 2: #28
151–153	Debris #10, Accident #1
156–157	Accident Turn 2: #23
159–160	Accident Turn 4: #10, #42, #46, #77

The Brickyard 400
DRIVER PROFILES

The first five years of the Brickyard 400 brought some of the greatest names in racing—from Petty and Earnhardt to Andretti and Foyt—to one of the most storied tracks in the world— the Indianapolis Motor Speedway. The following profiles and statistics offer an intimate look at the drivers who qualified for the first five races.

The Brickyard's most consistent driver: Bill Elliott.

Richard Petty made the Brickyard as a team owner.

Perennial threat Mark Martin.

A.J. Foyt made the inaugural field at the Brickyard 400.

Junior Johnson and Jimmy Spencer.

John Andretti kept his namesake's legacy alive.

Davey Allison drove at Indy for the 1992 test.

Of all the names to enter the gates of Indianapolis Motor Speedway, few are better known to the fans than Andretti. And when speaking of the Brickyard 400, it is John Andretti who takes center stage.

Like his famous relatives Mario and Michael Andretti, the Indianapolis native knew what he wanted to do with his life from the time he could walk. Driving fast (in various forms of motorsports) was all he ever contemplated. After stints in open-wheel Indy cars and drag racing, John decided in 1994 to make NASCAR racing his chosen profession. This occurred 27 years after his Uncle Mario first entered NASCAR and was victorious in the 1967 Daytona 500.

The year that John Andretti found his home with NASCAR was also the first time stock cars graced the famed 2.5-mile facility. Andretti entered a Chevrolet owned by Billy Hagan, the same owner who fielded Terry Labonte for his first Winston Cup championship in 1984. Like any driver, Andretti had to adjust to the heavier stock cars but managed to start the 1994 Brickyard 400 in 28th and finish in the same position, two laps off the pace.

Few NASCAR drivers can appreciate the tradition and aura of the Indianapolis Motor Speedway like John Andretti. The nephew of 1969 Indy 500 winner Mario Andretti ran the inaugural Brickyard 400 for owner Billy Hagan, was in the Michael Kranefuss-owned cars for the 1995 and 1996 races, drove for Cale Yarborough in 1997, and then drove for Richard Petty in 1998.

STP, which has always maintained a strong presence at the Memorial Day weekend Indianapolis 500, has had an equally-strong presence in the five Brickyard 400s. Wally Dallenbach Jr. drove the Richard Petty-owned No. 43 Pontiac in 1994, Bobby Hamilton in 1995, 1996, and 1997, then Indianapolis native John Andretti in 1998.

Year	Car #	Sponsor	Make	SP	FP	Laps	Reason Out	Laps Led	Prize Money
1994	14	Bryant/Byrd's Cafe	Chevy	28	28	158	Running	0	$39,000
1995	37	Kmart/Little Caesars	Ford	23	12	160	Running	6	$77,400
1996	37	Kmart/Little Caesars	Ford	27	19	160	Running	0	$72,460
1997	98	RCA	Ford	35	17	160	Running	0	$80,095
1998	43	STP	Pontiac	9	7	160	Running	0	$138,160
Total						798		6	$407,115

RON BARFIELD

Once a protégé to 1988 NASCAR Winston Cup champion Bill Elliott, Ron Barfield has engaged in various forms of NASCAR racing in hopes of gaining experience for a career in Winston Cup racing.

In 1997, Barfield started the Brickyard 400 from the 23rd position and finished one position higher in 22nd, on the lead lap.

Presently, Barfield continues to search for a competitive Winston Cup opportunity, remaining a strong contender in both the NASCAR Busch Series and NASCAR Truck Series.

Ron Barfield's only appearance at the Brickyard came in 1997.

Barfield drove the New Holland Ford for the 1997 race.

Year	Car #	Sponsor	Make	SP	FP	Laps	Reason Out	Laps Led	Prize Money
1997	92	New Holland	Ford	23	22	160	Running	0	$64,935

JOHNNY BENSON JR. 26

Even though he's only been in the NASCAR Winston Cup ranks for just over two and half years, Johnny Benson Jr. has wasted no time showing the stock car world he means business. The Michigan native is a former NASCAR Busch Series champion and the 1996 NASCAR Winston Cup Rookie of the Year.

In 1996, Benson spent the first half of the season learning the various track configurations and the handling characteristics of his Bahari Racing Pontiacs. And at Indianapolis, everything seemed to fall into place.

With the help of a pit strategy that called for two tire changes instead of four, Benson found himself at the front battling with crafty veterans who make winning look easy. He rolled away from them more than once by healthy margins and looked every bit the part of a Brickyard 400 winner.

Unfortunately, problems on a late-race pit stop took away all his chances for the win, relegating him to 8th. Despite the sting of losing the lead, Benson's high finish was a valuable learning experience as he discovered how competitive NASCAR Winston Cup racing can be.

In 1997, Benson shined again. He started the 160-lap event in 20th position, but that number was misleading, since his car had much more power than his qualifying position indicated. Taking the lead on Laps 41 and 81, he bested his 1996 performance by one position, ending up in 7th. At season's end, Benson was 11th in the point standings, which prompted team owner Jack Roush to hire him to drive his Fords in 1998.

Johnny Benson made his third Brickyard 400 appearance in 1998, this time in a Ford Taurus owned by Jack Roush.

Jack Roush fielded five cars in the 1998 Brickyard 400, including the Cheerios-sponsored No. 26 Ford Taurus for Johnny Benson. The team used a provisional to start 39th, then finished a lap down in 25th place.

Year	Car #	Sponsor	Make	SP	FP	Laps	Reason Out	Laps Led	Prize Money
1996	30	Pennzoil	Pontiac	14	8	160	Running	70	$166,485
1997	30	Pennzoil	Pontiac	20	7	160	Running	2	$121,760
1998	26	Cheerios	Ford	39	25	159	Running	0	$84,310
Total						479		72	$372,555

ED BERRIER

The son of longtime racer Max Berrier, Ed Berrier grew up working on race cars at his Winston-Salem, North Carolina, home. Races at the famed Bowman Gray Stadium occupied many Saturday nights in his formative years.

Following in his father's footsteps, Berrier drove first on the short tracks of North Carolina, South Carolina, and Virginia. In 1984, he started racing in the NASCAR Busch Series division and has been a mainstay ever since. On two occasions, he has started Winston Cup events. One of those came with a start in the 1997 Brickyard 400.

While driving a Chevrolet for Sadler Brothers Racing, Berrier qualified 30th and finished the prestigious event in 27th, one lap off the pace. Still, he was running at the finish and collected his biggest racing purse to date—$62,210.

In April 1998, Berrier collected his first NASCAR Busch Series victory at Martinsville, Virginia.

Busch Series mainstay Ed Berrier drove in the 1997 Brickyard only.

Berrier drove a Shoney's-sponsored Chevrolet and finished the race one lap down.

Year	Car #	Sponsor	Make	SP	FP	Laps	Reason Out	Laps Led	Prize Money
1997	95	Shoney's	Chevy	30	27	159	Running	0	$62,210

RICH BICKLE

Rich Bickle has driven some very strong equipment during his career. He came to Winston Cup racing from a dirt track in Jefferson, Wisconsin, where he racked up 230 short track wins. His first big-time start was at the Charlotte Motor Speedway in 1989, and he has made sporadic starts ever since.

An experienced driver in all three of NASCAR's major divisions, Bickle entered the Brickyard 400 for the first time in 1994 driving the Melling Racing Ford. He started in 19th position and ended 29th, completing 157 laps. In 1995, he switched over to a Pontiac sponsored by Kendall Motor Oils and owned by Felix Sabates. He started and ended the race in the same position—36th, with 154 laps completed.

In 1996, Bickle drove in the NASCAR Truck Series for Richard Petty and finished 11th in the annual standings. He did not enter the Brickyard 400 that year.

Bickle joined up with Darrell Waltrip's team in 1997 for truck racing and Winston Cup. Bickle finished second in the truck series point standings with three wins. He qualified 10th for the Brickyard 400 and was running an impressive race until an accident on Lap 153 forced him into a 34th-place finish.

In 1998, Bickle joined Cale Yarborough Motorsports after their primary driver Greg Sacks was injured at Texas Motor Speedway on April 5. Bickle stepped in, performed admirably, and kept the team's Fords competitive. He finished 39th in the 1998 Brickyard race. Bickle also has 14 NASCAR Busch Series starts to his credit.

Midwestern native Rich Bickle ran in the 1998 Brickyard 400 after injuries from a spring racing accident sidelined Cale Yarborough Motorsports driver Greg Sacks. Bickle has qualified for four of the five Brickyard 400s, missing only the 1996 race when he didn't have a ride.

The 1998 race was the third in which Cale Yarborough's team had a new sponsor: Fingerhut claimed sponsorship with Jeremy Mayfield in 1994, RCA with Mayfield in 1995 and 1996, then RCA with John Andretti in 1997, and Thorn Apple Valley with Rich Bickle in 1998.

Year	Car #	Sponsor	Make	SP	FP	Laps	Reason Out	Laps Led	Prize Money
1994	9	Orkin Pest Control	Ford	19	29	157	Running	0	$24,000
1995	40	Kendall	Pontiac	36	36	154	Running	0	$52,675
1997	26	KFC Team Twister	Chevy	10	34	153	Accident	0	$56,410
1998	98	Thorn Apple Valley	Ford	31	39	112	Running	0	$74,650
Total						576		0	$207,735

BRETT BODINE

Since late 1995, Brett Bodine has worn two hats in NASCAR Winston Cup racing—those of driver and team owner. Bodine entered the owner's arena when he bought his operation from legendary driver and owner Junior Johnson. (At the start of the 1998 season, Bodine sold half of the interest in his team to Andy Evans, and the new operation is now called Scandia Racing.)

Previous to donning his owner's cap, Bodine established himself as a successful NASCAR driver. Born in Elmira, New York, Bodine began his racing career driving hobby cars at Chemung Speedrome in 1977. His experience there led him into Modifieds from 1980 to 1984; this included winning the 1984 track championship at Stafford Motor Speedway (Connecticut).

Bodine first entered a Winston Cup event for team owner Rick Hendrick in 1986 at the Coca-Cola 600. The following year, Junior Johnson called on him as a relief driver for Terry Labonte during two events when the Texas native was injured. That led to 14 events with team owner Hoss Ellington. In 1988, he drove for well-known team owner Bud Moore.

From 1990 to 1994, Bodine was teamed with drag racer and Winston Cup team owner Kenny Bernstein. Bodine's first and only Winston Cup win so far came in 1990 at North Wilkesboro, North Carolina. In his final year with Bernstein, Bodine was determined to make a good showing in the Brickyard 400.

Brett Bodine finished second in the 1994 Brickyard 400 after driving away from a controversial accident with his older brother, Geoff. The middle of the three racing Bodine brothers has run all five Brickyard 400s, the first with owner Kenny Bernstein, the second with Junior Johnson, and the next three with his own No. 11 Ford team.

When Lowe's Home Improvement Warehouse left the Brett Bodine-owned team after the 1997 season, Bodine landed sponsorship from Paychex, a company that helps businesses with their payroll and benefits programs.

Year	Car #	Sponsor	Make	SP	FP	Laps	Reason Out	Laps Led	Prize Money
1994	26	Quaker State	Ford	7	2	160	Running	10	$203,575
1995	11	Lowe's	Ford	12	24	159	Running	0	$67,700
1996	11	Lowe's	Ford	22	22	159	Running	0	$69,160
1997	11	Close Call	Ford	42	18	160	Running	0	$79,535
1998	11	Paychex	Ford	40	33	152	Running	0	$75,535
Total						790		10	$495,505

GEOFF BODINE

Geoff Bodine has always been aware of the prestige the Brickyard gives to all of its winners. And as long as he can remember, Bodine has wanted to turn a few laps there— he just had no idea it would be in a stock car.

In August 1994, he was finally given the opportunity to drive the famed 2.5-mile oval. That first outing was disappointing. He enjoyed an impressive qualifying run and started from the 4th position but found himself in the wall on Lap 99 after being involved in an accident with his brother Brett.

In 1995, Bodine started the event from the 25th position and was running in the lead lap when he came across the finish line in 15th. In 1996, Bodine dropped five positions to finish 20th after starting 29th in the 40-car field.

Bodine hit his lowest point when he didn't qualify for the 1997 Brickyard 400. With speeds simply not fast enough to make the field, Bodine and company were forced to load up their Ford Thunderbird and return to their Harrisburg, North Carolina, shop.

Since August 1997, Geoff Bodine has been a new man. The Elmira, New York, native sold a large portion of his race team to co-owners Jim Mattei and John Porter. Almost immediately the team began to perform better with seven top-15 performances in 12 events to finish the season.

The best finish of Geoff Bodine's four Brickyard 400s (he didn't qualify for the 1997 race) was 15th in the second race. He was 39th in the inaugural race in 1994, 15th the next year, 20th in the 1996 race, and 37th in the 1998 event.

Geoff Bodine qualified 13th—one of his best efforts of the year—but finished 37th in the 1998 Brickyard 400. His Philips Consumer Electronics No. 7 Ford suffered handling problems in a multi-car accident.

Year	Car #	Sponsor	Make	SP	FP	Laps	Reason Out	Laps Led	Prize Money
1994	7	Exide Batteries	Ford	4	39	99	Accident	24	$45,600
1995	7	Exide Batteries	Ford	25	15	160	Running	0	$79,400
1996	7	QVC	Ford	29	20	160	Running	0	$73,160
1998	7	Philips Communications	Ford	13	37	124	Vibration	0	$74,745
Total						543		24	$272,905

TODD BODINE

Todd Bodine, the youngest of the Bodine brothers, has made several changes in his career recently.

He began the 1998 NASCAR Winston Cup season with team owner Bob Hancher but was released in July because of problems the team suffered while attempting to qualify for races. Bodine is presently back in the NASCAR Busch Series ranks with Team 34 Racing. But in the past, he has enjoyed a couple stellar runs at the Brickyard.

In 1994, Bodine started the event in 25th and finished 9th for team owner Butch Mock. The next year, he finished 21st after improving his position from 34th. His Ford Thunderbird was one lap down to the leaders when he completed his race.

Bodine did not qualify for either the 1996 or 1997 Brickyard 400. He did not attempt to qualify for the 1998 Brickyard 400.

Todd Bodine was one of three Bodine brothers in the inaugural Brickyard 400 in 1994. Driving for owner Butch Mock, he started 25th and finished a lead-lap 9th. He returned in 1995 with Mock (started 34th, finished 21st) but didn't have a ride for the 1996, 1997, or 1998 races.

The inaugural Brickyard 400 was good to Todd Bodine and team owner Butch Mock. They qualified their Ford Thunderbird 25th, then finished a lead-lap 9th, a performance worth $63,600.

Year	Car #	Sponsor	Make	SP	FP	Laps	Reason Out	Laps Led	Prize Money
1994	75	Factory Stores of Amer.	Ford	25	9	160	Running	1	$63,600
1995	75	Factory Stores of Amer.	Ford	34	21	159	Running	0	$66,300
Total						319		1	$129,900

GEOFF BRABHAM

A driver from Sydney, Australia, whose fame has come in the open wheeled Indy car ranks, Geoff Brabham has only one career start in NASCAR Winston Cup competition. That start came in the 1994 Brickyard 400, wheeling a Ford for team owners Carl Haas and Michael Kranefuss.

Brabham started the event from the 18th position and made several team owners take notice when he found his spot in the first-round qualifying. Overall, however, the outing didn't prove to be very favorable. Brabham was taken out of action in a crash that occurred on Lap 127. Brabham collected $27,400 for his efforts. He has yet to enter another NASCAR Winston Cup event.

Australian native Geoff Brabham landed a ride with rookie Winston Cup team owner Michael Kranefuss for the inaugural Brickyard 400 in 1994. An acknowledged star in sports car and Indy car racing, he qualified 18th and finished 38th in his first NASCAR race.

Geoff Brabham was involved in a single-car accident that eliminated him 127 laps into the 160-lap Brickyard 400 of 1994. He was driving a Ford Thunderbird for Michael Kranefuss, who was making his debut as a Winston Cup team owner.

Year	Car #	Sponsor	Make	SP	FP	Laps	Reason Out	Laps Led	Prize Money
1994	07	Kmart	Ford	18	38	127	Accident	0	$27,400

GARY BRADBERRY

A short track veteran from Alabama, Gary Bradberry has gained the attention of several veteran team owners as a future star in NASCAR Winston Cup racing.

Bradberry didn't enter the Brickyard 400 until 1996 when he drove a Ford for Sadler Brothers Racing. He started the event from the 26th position and finished 29th.

Bradberry didn't qualify for the 1997 or 1998 Brickyard 400 events.

Journeyman driver Gary Bradberry drove a Shoney's-backed No. 95 Ford Thunderbird in the 1996 Brickyard 400 but didn't make the field when he came back two years later in a Ford Taurus sponsored by Pilot Travel Centers.

Gary Bradberry didn't make the field for the 1998 Brickyard 400.

Year	Car #	Sponsor	Make	SP	FP	Laps	Reason Out	Laps Led	Prize Money
1996	95	Shoney's	Ford	26	29	158	Running	0	$54,935

JEFF BURTON

99

The South Boston, Virginia, native began driving go-karts at a very young age and later moved up to Pure Stock and Late Model divisions on short tracks in his home state. After several successful years in the Busch Series, Burton made his debut in NASCAR Winston Cup during 1994 with Stavola Brothers Racing.

Burton found the Indianapolis Motor Speedway to his liking during NASCAR's inaugural year at the famed 2.5-mile Brickyard. Burton started 38th and more than held his own to finish 19th.

In 1995, Burton's trip to the Brickyard didn't produce a great deal of happiness for him or his team. Mechanical problems sent him to the back of the 38-car pack. He finished the race 19 laps behind.

In 1996, Burton was determined to finally log an impressive finish. He joined team owner Jack Roush and had his best ride to date, starting 28th in the 40-car field. By race's end he had a hard fought 11th-place finish, which prompted others to noticed him as a potential winner.

In 1997, he started his Roush Racing Ford in 33rd and finished on the lead lap in the 15th position.

Burton had a rocket under his hood in 1998, but a mechanical problem dropped him 15 laps off the pace by race's end. Throughout the day, he continued running with the leaders, making up three of his lost laps.

Over the past two NASCAR Winston Cup seasons, Jeff Burton has been a regular contender from week to week, adding a new word to his vocabulary—consistency. In 1997, as driver of the No. 99 Roush Racing Ford, he finished 31 of the races in the 32-race schedule.

Jeff Burton is one of five drivers on the Jack Roush-owned team that fields Ford Tauruses. He has run all five Brickyard 400s (the first two with the Stavola Brothers, the last three with Roush), with finishes of 19th, 38th, 11th, 15th, and 36th.

Jeff Burton's Exide Batteries-backed No. 99 Ford Taurus started 34th and finished 36th in the 1998 Brickyard 400. Burton ran strong in the early laps but lost many laps while his crew made repairs to his transmission.

Year	Car #	Sponsor	Make	SP	FP	Laps	Reason Out	Laps Led	Prize Money
1994	8	Raybestos Douglas	Ford	38	19	159	Running	0	$41,600
1995	8	Raybestos	Ford	18	38	141	Running	0	$59,020
1996	99	Exide Batteries	Ford	28	11	160	Running	0	$82,260
1997	99	Exide Batteries	Ford	33	15	160	Running	21	$96,885
1998	99	Exide Batteries	Ford	34	36	145	Running	0	$84,385
Total						765		21	$364,150

WARD BURTON

Ward Burton's demeanor is as quiet and straightforward as his strong Virginia accent. And like his brother Jeff, this native southerner's early career featured go-kart, Pure Stock, and Late Model races as a child and teenager.

Burton found great success on the local level at the South Boston Speedway (Virginia), immediately becoming one of the best-liked drivers on every level that he's completed. He joined the NASCAR Busch Series division in 1990 where he logged four career victories.

Ward Burton's demeanor is Burton joined Winston Cup team owner Alan Dillard in 1994. That year, he began the inaugural Brickyard 400 in the 33rd position and bested it by only two spots, five laps off the pace.

With nine races remaining in the 1995 season, Burton joined team owner Bill Davis and won his first NASCAR Winston Cup race at North Carolina Speedway in Rockingham during October of that year. Two months earlier while still with Dillard's operation, Burton started the Brickyard 400 in 30th position and finished 35th, six laps off the pace.

In 1996, Burton began his third Brickyard 400 in the 32nd position and finished a disappointing 36th after suffering engine problems.

Burton's best year at the Brickyard came in 1997 when he started the race in 36th position and finished 19th, on the lead lap. In 1998 he started 34th and ended four places better in 30th place.

Virginia native Ward Burton drives the MBNA-sponsored No. 22 Pontiac Grand Prix for long-time team owner Bill Davis. He competed in the first two Brickyard 400s for Cale Yarborough Motorsports and the next three for Davis.

The No. 22 Bill Davis-owned Pontiac Grand Prix started 30th and finished 34th in the 1998 Brickyard 400. It was nine laps behind after running out of gas and coasting to a stop in Turn 3 near the midpoint of the 160-lap race.

Year	Car #	Sponsor	Make	SP	FP	Laps	Reason Out	Laps Led	Prize Money
1994	31	Hardee's	Chevy	33	31	155	Running	0	$23,500
1995	31	Hardee's	Chevy	30	35	154	Engine	0	$47,925
1996	22	MBNA America	Pontiac	32	36	82	Engine	0	$64,935
1997	22	MBNA America	Pontiac	36	19	160	Running	0	$78,435
1998	22	MBNA America	Pontiac	30	34	151	Running	0	$75,285
Total						702		0	$290,080

Mike Chase, a former NASCAR Winston West champion, raced in the NASCAR Winston Cup series from 1990 to 1994. During this time he competed in only 13 events, which included the 1994 Brickyard 400.

In that event, Chase started from the 43rd position but was involved in an accident with Dave Marcis on the 91st lap. Chase's Ford sustained heavy damage, and he was left to finish in 42nd, one position ahead of his start.

Chase has continued to compete in the NASCAR Truck Series since his lone Brickyard 400 start.

One of Mike Chase's sporadic appearances in Winston Cup races included the 1994 Brickyard.

Chase drove a Tyson Food's Chevrolet for 91 laps, until an accident ended his race.

Year	Car #	Sponsor	Make	SP	FP	Laps	Reason Out	Laps Led	Prize Money
1994	58	Tyson Foods	Chevy	43	42	91	Accident	0	$21,825

DERRIKE COPE

Of all the drivers who have made a career of NASCAR Winston Cup racing, there are few who have been as determined to be successful as Derrike Cope.

The son of a drag racing champion, Cope began his racing career on short tracks near his Spokane, Washington, home. In 1980, he became NASCAR's Late Model Sportsman Rookie of the Year. Several years later, in 1983, he won the championship in the same series. In 1984, he was Winston West Rookie of the Year and nearly won the series championship, missing it by only four points.

Cope first entered the Winston Cup arena in 1982 in the Winston West 500 at the now defunct Riverside, California, International Raceway. In 1989, he joined team owner Bob Whitcomb, and in 1990 he scored a surprise win in the Daytona 500, followed by a win at Dover Downs.

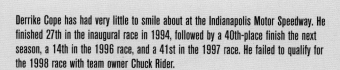
Derrike Cope has had very little to smile about at the Indianapolis Motor Speedway. He finished 27th in the inaugural race in 1994, followed by a 40th-place finish the next season, a 14th in the 1996 race, and a 41st in the 1997 race. He failed to qualify for the 1998 race with team owner Chuck Rider.

Derrike Cope missed the 1998 Brickyard 400 after scraping the wall in the second qualifying session. He wasn't fast enough to make the top 36 and didn't have enough team owner points to use a provisional.

Year	Car #	Sponsor	Make	SP	FP	Laps	Reason Out	Laps Led	Prize Money
1994	02	Children's Miracle Net	Ford	39	27	158	Running	0	$26,000
1995	12	Straight Arrow	Ford	37	40	104	Engine	0	$52,520
1996	12	Badcock	Ford	36	14	160	Running	0	$77,960
1997	36	Skittles	Pontiac	32	41	12	Accident	0	$55,755
Total						434		0	$212,235

RICKY CRAVEN

50

After several years of success on the short tracks of the Northeast and later the NASCAR Busch Series circuit, Craven—driving the Hendrick Motorsports Chevrolet—first entered the gates of the Indianapolis Motor Speedway in August 1995.

While driving for team owner Larry Hendrick, Craven found Indianapolis to his liking. The numbers don't show it, however, as Craven started 28th and dropped three positions to 31st, two laps behind the leaders.

Craven didn't improve very much in 1996. He began his quest for his first Brickyard 400 win in 39th but could do no better than 34th at the race's end. His Chevrolet suffered a broken rear-end pinion and could only complete 142 of the 160 laps.

Craven logged his best effort yet at Indianapolis in 1997. He started a dismal 41st but struggled all day, managing a 16th-place finish.

Injuries suffered later in 1997, including broken ribs, a broken shoulder, and inner ear problems, placed Craven on the sidelines. For a time, he voluntarily left the Hendrick Motorsports team during the 1998 season, but in his first race back, Craven scored the pole position at the New Hampshire International Raceway. The 1998 Brickyard 400 was Craven's third race back from his injury-induced layoff. He qualified an impressive 8th and finished 17th, on the lead lap.

Ricky Craven wasn't in Winston Cup when the inaugural Brickyard 400 was run in 1994. But he ran the 1995 and 1996 races with the Larry Hedrick-owned No. 41 Chevrolet team and the 1997 race in a Rick Hendrick-owned No. 25 Chevrolet. Despite some nagging health problems, he started 6th and finished a lead-lap 17th in the 1998 race in a No. 50 Hendrick-owned Chevrolet.

The 1998 Brickyard 400 was only Ricky Craven's third start after he returned from a self-imposed "medical leave" from the Hendrick Motorsports team. He qualified an impressive 6th and finished a lead-lap 17th in the 400-miler.

Year	Car #	Sponsor	Make	SP	FP	Laps	Reason Out	Laps Led	Prize Money
1995	41	Kodiak	Chevy	28	31	158	Running	0	$52,675
1996	41	Kodiak	Chevy	39	34	142	Engine	0	$57,435
1997	25	Budweiser	Chevy	41	16	160	Running	1	$82,135
1998	50	Budweiser	Chevy	6	17	160	Running	0	$92,810
Total						620		1	$285,055

WALLY DALLENBACH JR.

Like driver John Andretti, Wally Dallenbach has roots that are directly tied to the Indianapolis Motor Speedway. His father, Wally Dallenbach Sr., was once a top-name driver in Indy car racing. He won five events during his career and also worked as a CART official. More than once, Dallenbach Jr. found himself walking the grounds of the famed Brickyard or watching his father from the sidelines.

In 1991, Dallenbach came to NASCAR Winston Cup racing and joined team owner Junie Donlavey for 11 events. Some impressive finishes caught the eye of powerhouse team owner Jack Roush, who offered him a full-time ride for the 1992 and 1993 seasons. Dallenbach was given some road racing opportunities, with Roush promising success. But when it came to Winston Cup racing, the chemistry simply didn't produce wins in any of his 59 starts.

In 1994, Dallenbach got to turn laps at the Brickyard behind the wheel of the Petty Enterprises Pontiac. He posted a 22nd starting position but, after completing 159 laps, finished in 23rd position.

After completing only 14 of the scheduled 32 Winston Cup events of the 1994 season, Dallenbach elected to leave Petty Enterprises, saying the move would be best for the team. It was a mutual parting that showed the class Dallenbach possesses.

It wasn't until 1996 that Dallenbach returned to the Brickyard with longtime team owner Bud Moore.

Wally Dallenbach Jr. grew up around Indy car racing, which means the Indianapolis Motor Speedway has always held a special place in his heart. He's run in four of the five Brickyard 400s, missing only in 1995 when he didn't have a ride. He raced in the first one for Richard Petty, the 1996 race for veteran team owner Bud Moore, the 1997 race for Felix Sabates, and the 1998 race for NASCAR star Bill Elliott and NFL quarterback Dan Marino.

After starting 22nd, Wally Dallenbach Jr. managed only 102 of the 160 laps before the engine expired in his No. 13 Ford Taurus. He was credited with a 40th-place finish.

Year	Car #	Sponsor	Make	SP	FP	Laps	Reason Out	Laps Led	Prize Money
1994	43	STP	Pontiac	22	23	159	Running	0	$32,300
1996	15	Hayes Modems	Ford	18	17	160	Running	0	$74,660
1997	46	First Union	Chevy	14	36	120	Engine	14	$61,510
1998	13	First Plus Financial	Ford	22	40	102	Engine	0	$67,645
Total						541		14	$236,115

3

Without a doubt, seven-time NASCAR Winston Cup champion Dale Earnhardt is in a league all his own. For two decades, the Kannapolis, North Carolina, native has shattered the record books with racing accomplishments, intimidating the very best drivers in the process.

Inspired by his father, the late Ralph Earnhardt, he was immersed in stock car racing from an early age. Even though financing was hard to find at first, he continued to be successful on the short tracks of North Carolina and dabbled in the Winston Cup arena in the mid-1970s.

His big break came in 1979 when team owner Rod Osterland tapped him to drive the full Winston Cup schedule in hopes of winning Rookie of the Year honors, Earnhardt scaled that hurdle and went on to win his first Winston Cup championship in 1980.

Osterland sold Earnhardt's ride out from under him in 1981, prompting one of the most successful unions in NASCAR history. Richard Childress, a former driver, elected to turn car owner and put Earnhardt behind the wheel of his Pontiacs. The two enjoyed moderate success, but Childress didn't feel his equipment was good enough for such a stellar driver. The two split for two seasons, but joined forces again in 1984.

Their winning ways were nothing short of miraculous. The Earnhardt/Childress partnership accounts for 64 of Earnhardt's 71 NASCAR career victories, including the elusive 1998 Daytona 500 as well as six more championships. All told, Childress and Earnhardt have won over $31 million as a team.

The Indianapolis Motor Speedway has been good to them as well. Earnhardt was in strong contention to win the 1994 and 1996 races, and scored a victory in 1995. He also finished well in the 1998 race, moving up 23 spots to claim fifth place.

Seven-time NASCAR champion Dale Earnhardt has done well in four of his five Brickyard 400 appearances: 5th in the 1994 inaugural, 1st the next year, 15th in 1996 (with major relief help from Mike Skinner), and 5th in 1998. His only poor showing was 29th, two laps down, in the 1997 race.

Few sights on a NASCAR track are more threatening than the black No. 3 Chevrolet Monte Carlo when Dale Earnhardt is working his way toward the front of the pack.

Year	Car #	Sponsor	Make	SP	FP	Laps	Reason Out	Laps Led	Prize Money
1994	3	GM Goodwrench	Chevy	2	5	160	Running	2	$121,625
1995	3	GM Goodwrench	Chevy	13	1	160	Running	28	$565,600
1996	3	GM Goodwrench	Chevy	12	15	160	Running	1	$84,460
1997	3	GM Goodwrench	Chevy	5	29	158	Running	0	$76,310
1998	3	GM Goodwrench	Chevy	28	5	160	Running	6	$169,275
Total						798		37	$1,017,270

BILL ELLIOTT

For Bill Elliott, driver of his own Ford Taurus, the Brickyard 400 is still the missing jewel in his crown. In the first four Brickyard 400 events, Elliott finished among the top-10 cars. In the 1998 race, that didn't happen.

Since joining the NASCAR Winston Cup schedule in 1976, Elliott has enjoyed both great successes and the lowest of disappointments, but through it all, he continues to be a favorite of the fans. The Georgia native has been voted Winston Cup's "Most Popular Driver" 10 times and was Winston Cup champion in 1988. However, in 1995, he failed to win even one race.

By comparison, there have been few years as great as the one Elliott enjoyed in 1985. That year he won 11 races, including 3 of NASCAR's 4 biggest events and "The Winston Million," a special non-points event. His career winnings are well over $16 million and have been bolstered by four top-10 finishes in the Brickyard 400.

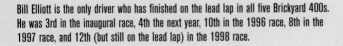
Bill Elliott is the only driver who has finished on the lead lap in all five Brickyard 400s. He was 3rd in the inaugural race, 4th the next year, 10th in the 1996 race, 8th in the 1997 race, and 12th (but still on the lead lap) in the 1998 race.

Although it's never won a race, the McDonald's-sponsored No. 94 Ford Taurus remains one of the most popular cars on the Winston Cup circuit.

Year	Car #	Sponsor	Make	SP	FP	Laps	Reason Out	Laps Led	Prize Money
1994	11	Budweiser/Amoco	Ford	6	3	160	Running	1	$164,850
1995	94	McDonald's	Ford	4	4	160	Running	47	$223,450
1996	94	McDonald's	Ford	7	10	160	Running	2	$98,585
1997	94	McDonald's	Ford	15	8	160	Running	0	$110,460
1998	94	McDonald's	Ford	37	12	160	Running	0	$102,110
Total						800		50	$699,455

A. J. FOYT

Of all the drivers who have walked down Gasoline Alley, none have known the Brickyard as intimately as A. J. Foyt. The Houston native logged four Indianapolis 500 victories during his Indy Car career. Just as Richard Petty is known as the King of the Daytona 500 because of his seven career victories there, Foyt is the Man at the Brickyard.

Early in his driving career, Foyt turned to stock cars to feed his urge to race. He won the Daytona 500 for the famed Wood Brothers (Glenn and Leonard) in 1972 and also logged six other victories in 128 total starts in NASCAR racing. He, along with Mario Andretti, are the only two drivers to win the biggest events in both Indy cars and stock cars.

Foyt's fascination with stock cars on the Indianapolis Motor Speedway prompted him to enter a car in the 1994 Brickyard 400. That year Foyt started 40th and moved his Ford up 10 positions by the finish. Since, Foyt has made several unsuccessful attempts at qualifying for the Brickyard 400.

What would a race at the Indianapolis Motor Speedway be without four-time Indy 500 winner A. J. Foyt? Super Tex started 40th and finished 30th in the first race but didn't make the field in his other attempts in 1995 and 1996.

Long-time sponsor Copenhagen was on the No. 50 Ford Thunderbird that A. J. Foyt drove in the inaugural Brickyard 400 in 1994. He ran as high as second until running out of gas, slowing and losing several laps.

Year	Car #	Sponsor	Make	SP	FP	Laps	Reason Out	Laps Led	Prize Money
1994	50	Copenhagen	Ford	40	30	156	Running	0	$29,000

HARRY GANT

As far as Harry Gant is concerned, there is a time and place for everything. When the Taylorsville, North Carolina, native began racing in the late 1960s, he decided he would retire at age 55, whether he was winning races or not. He turned 55 in 1994, and—as a man who holds true to his word—he retired.

Gant's early successes came on the short track, where his frequent victories earned him fans and respect. In 1973, he joined the NASCAR Winston Cup circuit. The popular driver entered 474 races and won 18 of them.

In his only Brickyard 400 start, Gant qualified 42nd, finishing 37th after experiencing mechanical problems. In the end, he completed 133 of the race's 160 laps.

Gant visits race tracks today to sign autographs but no longer drives in Winston Cup competition. He has, however, driven in some NASCAR Craftsman Truck Series races.

Harry Gant was one of NASCAR's most popular drivers, partly because he raced almost everywhere before joining the Winston Cup circuit and partly because he maintained an even keel through almost every circumstance. The 1994 Brickyard came deep into his farewell season in Winston Cup.

The familiar No. 33 "Skoal Bandit" of Harry Gant started 42nd, led a few laps during the first exchange of pit stops, then faded down the stretch and finished in 37th-place, 27 laps behind.

Year	Car #	Sponsor	Make	SP	FP	Laps	Reason Out	Laps Led	Prize Money
1994	33	Gas America/Skoal	Chevy	42	37	133	Running	1	$58,350

JEFF GORDON

There is a love affair going on between Jeff Gordon—driver of the Hendrick Motorsports Chevrolet—and the famed Indianapolis Motor Speedway.

You see, no other NASCAR driver enjoys the relationship Gordon has with the sacred Indiana speedway. He grew up just a few short miles from the track in Pittsboro and even met his idol Rick Mears there once. A decade later, it's Gordon who's now signing the autographs and a role model to small children all over the world.

Gordon stormed onto the NASCAR Winston Cup circuit in 1992, won the NASCAR Winston Cup Rookie of the Year honors, and proceeded to march toward his championship destiny.

From go-karts and micro midgets to the heavier, more monstrous Winston Cup cars, Gordon has adapted to them all. He has over 35 NASCAR Winston Cup wins, two career Winston Cup championships, and has collected nearly $19 million in winnings in just over six years. He is also the only driver to be heralded as a two-time winner of the Brickyard 400.

Many NASCAR watchers agree that Jeff Gordon and his Hendrick Motorsports team had the greatest impact on the unprecedented growth of Winston Cup in the United States during the mid-1990s. Young, personable, media- and sponsor-friendly, and enormously talented, the three-time series champion and two-time Brickyard 400 winner is widely considered the man best suited to lead stock car racing into the new millennium.

One of the most feared sights in all of NASCAR racing: the No. 24 Chevrolet Monte Carlo owned by Rick Hendrick, driven by Jeff Gordon, tuned by Ray Evernham, and sponsored by DuPont. It has won almost every meaningful Winston Cup race at least once, including two at the Indianapolis Motor Speedway.

Year	Car #	Sponsor	Make	SP	FP	Laps	Reason Out	Laps Led	Prize Money
1994	24	DuPont	Chevy	3	1	160	Running	93	$613,000
1995	24	DuPont	Chevy	1	6	160	Running	35	$299,200
1996	24	DuPont	Chevy	1	37	40	Accident	3	$137,591
1997	24	DuPont	Chevy	24	4	160	Running	25	$223,675
1998	24	DuPont	Chevy	3	1	160	Running	97	$1,637,625
Total						680		253	$2,911,091

ROBBY GORDON

Robby Gordon really has no preference when it comes to the type of racing machine he drives. The Orange, California, native will gladly slide down into an open-wheel Indy car or strap himself into a towering off-road racer, where he has won championships. He also races Winston Cup stock cars.

For a brief time, Gordon was a protégé of sorts to seven-time NASCAR Winston Cup champion Dale Earnhardt. He fielded cars for Earnhardt, as well as for team owner Felix Sabates who financed Gordon's 1997 run in the Indianapolis 500.

To date, Gordon has only entered one Brickyard 500, that being the 1997 race. He started the race in 11th position and finished 28th, one lap off the pace.

The "other" Gordon didn't fare well in his short-lived NASCAR career. Off-road and Indy car star Robby Gordon drove briefly for Junie Donlavey in 1991 and Robert Yates in 1993 before going to Sabco Racing in 1997. Gordon ran 20 of the year's 32 races, started at the pole position in the spring near Atlanta, but had just one top five and ended the disappointing season 40th in points.

Robby Gordon put the Felix Sabates-owned number 40 car through an erratic 1997 race. Gordon returned to the Indianapolis Motor Speedway for the 1998 Brickyard 400 with the No. 19 Yellow Freight Line Ford team, but failed to qualify for the race.

Year	Car #	Sponsor	Make	SP	FP	Laps	Reason Out	Laps Led	Prize Money
1997	40	Coors Light	Chevy	11	28	159	Running	0	$68,910

96

David Green of Owensboro, Kentucky, spent the first 3 years of the Brickyard 400 watching from the sidelines. He was trying to build a NASCAR Busch Series career. In 1994, the inaugural year of the Brickyard 400, Green was the Busch Series champion while driving for Winston Cup driver Bobby Labonte. Green finished 2nd in the series championship standings in 1996.

In 1997, Green did get into the Brickyard 400 line-up driving the Buzz McCall-owned Chevrolet Monte Carlo. He enjoyed a solid qualifying effort, starting in 9th position but experienced engine problems after 137 of the scheduled 160 laps and finished in 35th position.

Green returned to the NASCAR Busch Series this past June after parting company with McCall's Charlotte-based team.

The affable David Green's only Brickyard was in the 1997 race, where he qualified strongly but failed to finish.

Green drove the No. 96 Caterpillar Chevy for 137 laps before an accident ended his day.

Year	Car #	Sponsor	Make	SP	FP	Laps	Reason Out	Laps Led	Prize Money
1997	96	Caterpillar	Chevy	9	35	137	Accident	0	$56,160

JEFF GREEN

46

Like his older brother David Green, Jeff Green has had his sights on the NASCAR Winston Cup circuit since the days of running short tracks around his Owensboro, Kentucky, home.

Also like his brother, Jeff didn't get his first shot at running the Brickyard 400 until 1997. Driving for team owner Gary Bechtel, Green started the event in 26th and finished only one spot higher in 25th. As he passed the checkered flag to complete his run, Green found himself one lap down on the leaders. Still, his effort wasn't bad considering he was a rookie at the Indianapolis Motor Speedway.

In 1998, Green started the race from the 5th qualifying position, but late in the race, he was involved in an accident with Joe Nemechek that left him in the 30th finishing position, three laps off the pace.

Kentucky native Jeff Green began the 1998 NASCAR season driving for Winston Cup team owner Gary Bechtel. When Bechtel chose to concentrate on his two-team Busch Series stable, Green moved to the Felix Sabates-owned team as Wally Dallenbach's successor. His two older brothers—Mark and David—are full-schedule Busch Series drivers.

Jeff Green started an impressive 5th for Sabco Racing and finished 30th, three laps behind in the 1998 Brickyard 400. In his 1997 Indianapolis Motor Speedway debut for team owner Gary Bechtel, he started 26th and finished 25th.

Year	Car #	Sponsor	Make	SP	FP	Laps	Reason Out	Laps Led	Prize Money
1997	29	Cartoon Network	Chevy	26	25	159	Running	0	$67,735
1998	46	The Money Store	Chevy	5	30	157	Running	0	$69,785
Total						316		0	$137,520

41

Steve Grissom has often said if he wasn't a driver in NASCAR Winston Cup racing, then he would be doing all he could to get into the sport.

His desire to drive stock cars came from watching his father race on dirt tracks near his Gadsden, Alabama, home. Aside from showing his talents at high school football and basketball, Grissom began turning a few steering wheels of his own in the mid-1980s.

In 1990, Grissom started his first NASCAR Winston Cup event for team owner Dick Moroso. He finished out of the top 10 but was still impressive in his first start.

His next opportunity didn't come until 1993 when he was tapped by team owner Gary Bechtel. The union produced a full schedule for the next two seasons. Grissom logged six top-10 finishes for the fledgling team.

Grissom didn't find the speed he needed to qualify for the 1994 Brickyard 400. But in 1995, he qualified 39th in the 41-car field and was able to put together a 30th-place finish, two laps off the pace.

In 1996, Grissom and Bechtel parted ways, so Grissom did not enter the Brickyard 400. He joined team owner Larry Hendrick in 1997, giving his career a huge boost. Beginning with a 19th-place qualifying position, Grissom finished the Brickyard 400 in 26th, one lap off the leaders. In 1998, Grissom started the event in 28th and finished 23rd on the lead lap.

An outstanding high -school football player in Gadsden, Alabama, Steve Grissom turned down several scholarship offers to go racing. He was the 1985 NASCAR All-Pro and 1993 Busch Series champion, making his full-schedule Winston Cup debut in 1994 and finishing second to Jeff Burton in the Rookie of the Year competition.

The good news for Steve Grissom was that he finished on the lead lap in the 1998 Brickyard 400. The bad news was that 22 other lead-lap drivers were ahead of him, more evidence that Winston Cup is the world's most competitive racing series.

Year	Car #	Sponsor	Make	SP	FP	Laps	Reason Out	Laps Led	Prize Money
1994	55	Bondo/Mar-Hyde	Ford	24	32	155	Running	0	$23,000
1995	22	MBNA America	Pontiac	35	32	158	Running	0	$56,175
1998	41	Kodiak	Chevrolet	26	23	160	Running	0	$86,210
Total						473		0	$165,385

As a child, Bobby Hamilton watched his father and grandfather build NASCAR Winston Cup racers for legendary country music singer Marty Robbins. These fond memories set the stage for Hamilton's own driving aspirations.

Hamilton started gaining recognition in his home state of Tennessee when he became the 1988 Nashville Speedway track champion. That same year, he found himself driving a match race with Darrell Waltrip, Sterling Marlin, and Bill Elliott. To everyone's surprise, Hamilton won that race and opened a lot of eyes in the world of stock cars.

Rick Hendrick, owner of the powerful teams that have Jeff Gordon and Terry Labonte as drivers, also noticed Hamilton when drivers were being recruited for the movie *Days of Thunder*. Hendrick was a major consultant and provider of equipment for the film. He received a good word about Hamilton from three-time Winston Cup champion Darrell Waltrip. Both knew Hamilton had the potential to become a great NASCAR driver.

They were right. In his first Winston Cup event in 1989, Hamilton finished 5th at Phoenix International Raceway.

Hamilton's first full-time season came in 1991 as he won NASCAR Rookie of the Year honors with team owner George Bradshaw. But even bigger things were just around the corner.

Hamilton joined team owner Felix Sabates in 1994, and in 1995, Hamilton began the first year of a great relationship with Petty Enterprises and racing legend Richard Petty.

Hamilton captured his first career NASCAR victory at Phoenix in 1996. In 1997, he he logged his second career NASCAR victory. In 1998, Hamilton joined team owner Larry McClure.

In 1987, Bobby Hamilton was a successful Busch Series driver looking toward Winston Cup. He got there sooner than expected because of a strong run at Phoenix while helping team owner Rick Hendrick and Paramount film *Days of Thunder*. After two full seasons with George Bradshaw, one with Felix Sabates, and three with Richard Petty (getting his first two Cup victories), he moved to Morgan-McClure for 1998 and promptly won the spring race at Martinsville.

Bobby Hamilton's 20th place in the 1998 Brickyard 400 matched his second-best finish in his five Indianapolis Motor Speedway appearances (his best finish was 11th in 1995). He's completed all but five of the possible 800 laps in the five 160-lap races.

Year	Car #	Sponsor	Make	SP	FP	Laps	Reason Out	Laps Led	Prize Money
1994	40	Kendall Oil	Pontiac	32	24	159	Running	0	$35,200
1995	43	STP	Pontiac	2	11	160	Running	1	$89,000
1996	43	STP	Pontiac	37	31	156	Running	0	$58,435
1997	43	STP	Pontiac	12	20	160	Running	0	$82,935
1998	4	Kodak Film	Chevy	24	20	160	Running	0	$95,960
Total						795		1	$361,530

JIMMY HENSLEY

22

Jimmy Hensley has been one of NASCAR's mainstay drivers, dating back to 1968. For over three decades, Jimmy Hensley has been content to race whatever car has been available to him. He is best known for his ability to fill in when a team is experiencing adversity. By pinch hitting for various teams he has been able to pull them up when they needed a boost.

After a long string of short track events, which included a few sporadic visits to Winston Cup racing, Hensley was finally tapped for a full-time ride with Cale Yarborough Motorsports in 1990.

In 1994, Hensley entered the Brickyard 400 with team owner Diane DeWitt, qualifying the team's Ford in 24th and finishing 32nd.

His next appearance came with Bill Davis in 1995 when he qualified 35th and finished 32nd. As of 1998, he has not entered any other Brickyard 400 event.

Long-time Cup competitor Jimmy Hensley made two Brickyard appearances and finished 32nd both times.

Shown is the MBNA Pontiac Hensley drove in the 1995 race.

Year	Car #	Sponsor	Make	SP	FP	Laps	Reason Out	Laps Led	Prize Money
1994	55	Bondo/Mar-Hyde	Ford	24	32	155	Running	0	$23,000
1995	22	MBNA America	Pontiac	35	32	158	Running	0	$56,175
Total						313		0	$79,175

BOBBY HILLIN JR.

Bobby Hillin Jr. has been a fixture in NASCAR since first breaking into the Winston Cup ranks in the early 1980s under the direction of Harry Hyde, a stellar crew chief who took the late Bobby Isaac, Geoff Bodine, and the late Tim Richmond to their greatest triumphs. In 1986, Hillin, under Hyde's tutelage, captured his only Winston Cup victory, with Stavola Brothers Racing. (Hyde passed away in 1996 after suffering a heart attack.)

In 1994, Hillin started the Brickyard 400 with Huberczek Racing in the 35th position. He managed a 21st-place finish, one lap off the pace. The following year he was happy with his 17th-place start, but engine failure relegated him back to 39th after only 107 laps.

In 1996, Hillin came back to log an impressive 5th-place qualifying effort but fell to 26th, again one lap off the pace.

Hillin struggled in 1997 and left Winston Cup racing to compete in the NASCAR Busch Series.

Bobby Hillin Jr. grew up around Indy car racing—his father was a long-time sponsor and owner—but cast his lot with NASCAR as a high school student in Midland, Texas. He got his only victory in 1986 at Talladega as a teammate with Bobby Allison. He never ran a Brickyard 400 with the Heilig-Meyers livery but was with the team for the August 1993 test that helped Winston Cup teams get ready for the 1994 race. He drove that race for owner Charles Hardy and the 1995 and 1996 races for Doug Bawel.

Hillin drove Fords in all of his three appearances, two of those in the No. 77 Jasper-sponsored car (the 1995 version of that car is pictured).

Year	Car #	Sponsor	Make	SP	FP	Laps	Reason Out	Laps Led	Prize Money
1994	44	Buss Fuses	Ford	35	21	159	Running	0	$32,000
1995	77	Jasper Engines/US Air	Ford	17	39	107	Engine	1	$47,920
1996	77	Jasper Engines	Ford	5	26	159	Running	0	$54,935
Total						425		1	$134,855

36

Of all the drivers who have found success in NASCAR Winston Cup racing, Ernie Irvan—driver of the Nelson Bowers Racing Pontiac—has seen both the exhilarating glory of being on top and the painful depths of being at the very bottom of a sports career.

The California native started the 1994 Brickyard 400 in 17th but moved up and was holding the lead with only a few laps remaining when he cut a front tire on his Robert Yates Racing Ford, handing the win to Jeff Gordon. He end up finishing in the same position he started in, 17th.

Just two weeks after his Brickyard run, Irvan cut another tire in practice at Michigan International Speedway. He hit the wall, and the severity of the impact left him with only a 10-percent chance of surviving. But survive he did, missing 14 months on the racing circuit while recovering from his injuries. He was not able to enter the 1995 Brickyard 400, but later that year, he entered a race at North Wilkesboro, North Carolina—his first after the crash—and finished 6th while wearing an eye patch.

In 1996, Irvan returned to the Brickyard stronger than ever. Still with Robert Yates, Irvan qualified 15th in the 40-car field and finished a strong 2nd behind teammate Dale Jarrett after being passed in the final laps.

In 1997, Irvan placed his black, yellow, and red Ford on the pole position for the Brickyard 400 but had to settle for 10th on the lead lap.

In 1998, Irvan started on the pole position again for team owner Bowers. At race's end, he was still a strong 6th.

Ernie Irvan has had one of NASCAR's most eventful careers. After several years with teams that couldn't showcase his talent, he spent two seasons and part of two others with Morgan-McClure. He went to Robert Yates Racing after Davey Allison was killed, survived a life-threatening crash in 1994, then spent two-plus years at RYR before going to the Nelson Bowers-owned No. 36 Pontiac team for the 1998 season.

If the Indianapolis Motor Speedway owes anyone a Brickyard 400 victory, it's Ernie Irvan. A cut tire cost him the 1994 race. He was 2nd to teammate Dale Jarrett in 1996, won the pole and finished 10th in 1997, then started from the pole again and finished 6th in the 1998 race.

Year	Car #	Sponsor	Make	SP	FP	Laps	Reason Out	Laps Led	Prize Money
1994	28	Texaco/Havoline	Ford	17	17	159	Running	11	$52,000
1996	28	Texaco/Havoline	Ford	15	2	160	Running	39	$287,285
1997	28	Texaco/Havoline	Ford	1	10	160	Running	39	$143,560
1998	36	Skittles	Pontiac	1	6	160	Running	25	$159,260
Total						639		114	$642,105

KENNY IRWIN, JR. 28

Kenny Irwin, driver of the Robert Yates Racing Ford, enjoyed NASCAR Winston Cup racing on a full-time basis for the first time in 1998. In years past, the Indianapolis native cut his racing teeth in open-wheel midget machines with the United States Auto Club. In that division, he registered 8 wins and 20 runner-up finishes in five full seasons, starting in 1991.

Irwin also earned seven career USAC Sprint Car Series triumphs, as well as Rookie of the Year honors, in 1994 and a 2nd-place finish in the 1995 points standings. In addition, he was named Rookie of the Year in 1997's NASCAR Truck Series. He ended his season 10th in the final standings.

In his first start at the Brickyard 400 in 1998, Irwin began in 4th and put together an impressive run throughout the day. He was building toward a solid top-five finish when he lost control of his Ford, eventually finishing 38th.

Skeptics scoffed in the summer of 1997 when word spread that Sprint Car, Midget, and Craftsman Series driver Kenny Irwin would succeed Ernie Irvan at Robert Yates Racing. But nobody scoffed when Irwin qualified 2nd and finished 8th in his Winston Cup debut at Richmond in the fall of 1997. He continued that run in 1998, easily winning Rookie of the Year honors.

Hometown favorite Kenny Irwin qualified a stunning 4th for his first Brickyard 400 in 1998. He was running among the top 10 when he crashed, finishing 38th after 116 of the 160 laps.

Year	Car #	Sponsor	Make	SP	FP	Laps	Reason Out	Laps Led	Prize Money
1998	28	Texaco/Havoline	Ford	4	38	116	Accident	0	$98,805

DALE JARRETT

The Newton, North Carolina, native enjoyed his best season in 1997 with seven victories, losing the NASCAR Winston Cup championship by only 14 points. This momentum carried over to 1998 as well, with Jarrett in the running each week.

In Indianapolis, there has been a lot of glory to enjoy. Of the drivers who have entered all five Brickyard 400s to date, Dale Jarrett, who pilots the Robert Yates Racing Ford, has been a solid contender for the win each and every time.

Of all his Indy starts, the 1994 Brickyard 400 was the least kind to him. Jarrett started the 160-lap event in 14th position for team owner Joe Gibbs. An accident on Lap 99 left him on the sidelines.

In 1995, Jarrett joined Robert Yates, qualified 26th in a Ford, and by race's end posted a strong 3rd-place finish.

Everything came together for Jarrett in 1996 as he won over teammate Ernie Irvan; both were driving Robert Yates Fords. Jarrett started 24th and methodically worked his way toward the front. He led twice for only 11 laps, but they were the ones that counted.

In 1997, Jarrett started 3rd and was a strong contender before finishing in the same position.

In 1998, Jarrett was strong, at one point holding a 4.2-second lead. But near the halfway point his Ford ran dry of fuel, costing him four laps. With the help of caution flags, he came back to the lead lap, but time ran out too quickly to recover the win. It was a costly occurrence on the track and for the team's pocketbook, since they lost a $1-million special bonus they could have collected with a victory. Jarrett eventually finished 16th.

Dale Jarrett is among the handful of Winston Cup drivers who followed their fathers into racing. He spent several years on the Late Model and Busch Series tours before graduating to Cale Yarborough Motorsports, Wood Brothers Racing, and Joe Gibbs Racing. He's been with Robert Yates Racing since 1996, the year he won the third annual Brickyard 400.

An embarrassing mid-race fuel miscalculation cost Robert Yates Racing and driver Dale Jarrett a chance to win their second Brickyard 400 in 1998. After starting 2nd, Jarrett was leading at halfway when he ran out of gas at the start-finish line. He came from four laps down to finish 16th, but it was small consolation for the team many experts said would win the race.

Year	Car #	Sponsor	Make	SP	FP	Laps	Reason Out	Laps Led	Prize Money
1994	18	Interstate Batteries	Chevy	14	40	99	Accident	0	$33,225
1995	28	Texaco Havoline	Ford	26	3	160	Running	0	$203,200
1996	88	Quality Care	Ford	24	1	160	Running	11	$564,035
1997	88	Quality Care	Ford	3	3	160	Running	31	$223,900
1998	88	Quality Care	Ford	2	16	160	Running	27	$140,260
Total						739		69	$1,164,620

BUCKSHOT JONES

When Roy "Buckshot" Jones began racing stock cars in 1991, he quickly established himself as a driver with star potential. However, even after taking up racing, he continued working toward a degree in business at the University of Georgia. Once his studies were complete and his diploma was in hand, he worked harder toward his next goal—making a name for himself in NASCAR.

Jones joined the All Pro Series in 1993 and moved to the Busch Series in 1995 where he established himself as a front runner. When he came to the Winston Cup series in 1998, he drove for his father, Billy Jones, rather than accept offers from several more established teams.

Don't call him Roy. It's Buckshot, as in Buckshot Jones, one of the Busch Series' most flamboyant and exciting young drivers. In preparation for chasing 1999 Winston Cup Rookie of the Year honors, the University of Georgia grad brought his family-owned car to the 1998 Brickyard 400.

Jones drove the No. 00 Realtree Chevrolet for the 1998 Brickyard 400.

Year	Car #	Sponsor	Make	SP	FP	Laps	Reason Out	Laps Led	Prize Money
1998	00	Real Tree Extra	Chevy	15	27	158	Running	0	$72,285

BOBBY LABONTE

One might say that Bobby Labonte has had a love-hate relationship with Indianapolis Motor Speedway. As driver of the Joe Gibbs Racing Pontiac, Labonte has either been impressive in qualifying and race performance or quite frustrated with the final finishing order.

Like his older brother Terry Labonte, the younger Texan is hungry for wins and has scored at least one victory during the past four seasons. All told, he's collected seven career wins—all with Gibbs.

Labonte entered the 1994 Brickyard 400 in the Bill Davis Racing Pontiac in the 5th starting position but had to settle for 16th-place finish on the lead lap.

A year later, Labonte started 5th again, this time driving for former National Football League coach Joe Gibbs. Once again, he posted a strong run in the lead lap throughout the day and gave Gibbs his first impressive finish at the Brickyard, a 9th.

In 1996, Labonte struggled terribly. Starting 23rd in his apple green Chevrolet, he could only muster a 24th-place finish, one lap behind the leaders.

In 1997, less than 1 second separated Labonte from Ricky Rudd's 1st-place Ford. Labonte was in contention all day and put together a strong late-race run.

Labonte enjoyed another strong day in 1998 with a top-five finish. He was in the hunt for the win in the closing stages but was passed by both Jeff Gordon and Mark Martin.

After being recognized throughout much of his racing career as Terry's little brother, Bobby Labonte has begun to emerge from the two-time Winston Cup champion's shadow. Bobby went from Late Models and Busch Series cars to Winston Cup, where he was second to Jeff Gordon for 1993 Rookie of the Year. He raced the 1993 and 1994 seasons for Bill Davis and has been with Joe Gibbs Racing for the past four seasons.

After being 2nd to Ricky Rudd in the 1997 Brickyard 400, Bobby Labonte was 3rd behind Jeff Gordon and Mark Martin in the 1998 race. He was 16th in the 1994 inaugural race, 9th in the 1995 race, and 24th in the 1996 race. He's completed 799 of the 800 laps in his five appearances.

Year	Car #	Sponsor	Make	SP	FP	Laps	Reason Out	Laps Led	Prize Money
1994	22	Maxwell House Coffee	Pontiac	5	16	160	Running	0	$43,800
1995	18	Interstate Batteries	Chevy	5	9	160	Running	2	$99,500
1996	18	Interstate Batteries	Chevy	23	24	159	Running	0	$72,960
1997	18	Interstate Batteries	Pontiac	25	2	160	Running	0	$242,275
1998	18	Interstate Batteries	Pontiac	10	3	160	Running	2	$224,525
Total						799		4	$683,060

TERRY LABONTE

Terry Labonte, driver of the Hendrick Motorsports Chevrolet, has been called the "Ice Man." He got that name because of his quiet, icy demeanor and his ability to battle through the toughest situations on the race track. For example, many thought the career of this Texas native was close to over in 1993 when he had a lackluster year with team owner Billy Hagan. But then fellow driver Ricky Rudd announced he would field his own team for the 1994 Winston Cup season. This left a void at Hendrick Motorsports—which was filled by Labonte, giving his career new life. The 1984 NASCAR champion had wind in his sails again for the first time in nearly five years.

Labonte started the 1994 Brickyard 400 in 21st position but had to settle for a 12th-place finish on the lead lap. He did score three other wins that year, however, including his first trip to victory lane since 1989.

In 1995 Labonte struggled with his start and finish positions. He started the Brickyard race in 15th position moving up only two places to finish 13th. The following year, Labonte found some magic, starting in 9th position and coming in 3rd overall.

Then came 1997—a year nothing seemed to go well. Labonte qualified in 38th but had to settle for a disappointing 40th-place finish after suffering engine problems after 83 laps. In 1998, Labonte improved greatly, qualifying 8th and finishing 9th on the lead lap.

They call 1984 and 1996 Winston Cup champion Terry Labonte the "Iceman" because he's so cool and detached under pressure. Shy, quiet, and self-effacing almost to a fault, the native Texan holds the NASCAR record for most consecutive starts (602 as of the end of 1998). He's won at least one points race in 13 of the 20 full seasons he's been in Winston Cup, the last five of them with Hendrick Motorsports.

After starting eighth, Terry Labonte drove a smart and opportunistic race to finish ninth in the 1998 Brickyard 400. He's one of only a handful of drivers to have run all five Brickyard 400s with the same sponsorship package.

Year	Car #	Sponsor	Make	SP	FP	Laps	Reason Out	Laps Led	Prize Money
1994	5	Kellogg's	Chevy	21	12	160	Running	0	$57,500
1995	5	Kellogg's	Chevy	15	13	160	Running	0	$80,500
1996	5	Kellogg's	Chevy	9	3	160	Running	8	$209,535
1997	5	Kellogg's	Chevy	38	40	83	Engine	1	$77,755
1998	5	Kellogg's	Chevy	8	9	160	Running	0	$133,135
Total						723		9	$558,425

CHAD LITTLE

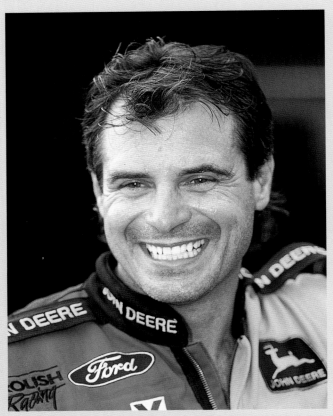

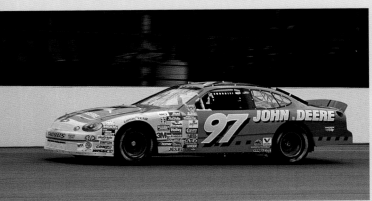

Chad Little, driver of the Roush Racing Ford, first directed his career ambitions toward law and marketing. In fact, he holds college degrees in both these fields. But, for now, his racing aspirations have won out.

While he was still a teenager, he began racing on the short tracks around Spokane, Washington. In 1981, he won the Late Model championship at Spokane Speedway, marking the beginning of a long rewarding career in racing.

By 1986, Little got the opportunity to drive in two Winston Cup events and did so sporadically over the next four years. His schedule increased with various team owners, such as Cale Yarborough and Harry Melling, from 1988 until 1991 when he first fielded his own team. Little also joined former NFL quarterback Mark Rypien for both the NASCAR Busch Series and Winston Cup.

Late in the 1997 NASCAR Winston Cup season, Little began talking with Roush about joining forces with his five-car Winston Cup effort. A deal was struck and Little's Mark Rypien Motorsports Pontiacs were quickly changed to Ford Tauruses. This same year Little ran in his first Brickyard 400 with a less than impressive showing. He worked hard to start the 160-lap race in 22nd position, but an accident dropped him to 42nd in the 43-car field after completing only two laps.

Little entered the 1998 Brickyard 400 in Jack Roush's car, the best ride of his 11-year career. He finished 28th after starting the race from the 35th position.

Chad Little has a marketing degree from Washington State University and a law degree from Gonzaga University but would rather be racing than anything else. He debuted in Winston Cup in 1986, running his first full season in 1991. After getting knocked around in Cup for several years, he backed up and regrouped by running the 1995, 1996, and 1997 Busch Series schedule, winning six races and finishing three straight years among the top five in points. In 1998, he rejoined the Cup Series, signing on with Jack Roush Racing.

The Indianapolis Motor Speedway hasn't been especially kind to Chad Little. He finished only 2 of 160 laps before crashing out in 1997, then started 35th and finished 28th in the 1998 race.

Year	Car #	Sponsor	Make	SP	FP	Laps	Reason Out	Laps Led	Prize Money
1997	97	John Deere	Pontiac	21	42	2	Accident	0	$55,755
1998	97	John Deere	Ford	35	28	157	Accident	0	$73,985
Total						159		0	$129,740

DAVE MARCIS

Dave Marcis, driver of his own NASCAR Winston Cup Chevrolets, is known as the last of the "old time independents"—those who do not depend on financial backing from the automakers. Marcis, who began his career in 1968, has held on through some very trying times and some very low bank accounts and has gained the support of fans who regularly pull for the underdog.

During his days of driving equipment for other team owners, he scored four career victories, as well as scoring one victory with his own team. Those victories came some 16 years ago, but even so, Marcis has continued on, hoping for another elusive victory. Even though his chances of winning the Brickyard 400 have been slim against the highly financed teams, he continues to enter the race and simply enjoys being part of the show.

As long as the 57-year-old Wisconsin native feels good and competitive, he plans to continue racing.

At 55 years of age, Dave Marcis is one of the most enduring figures in NASCAR Winston Cup racing. He moved south from Wisconsin in 1968 and has been to almost every race ever since. His glory years were the 1970s when he drove for Roger Penske, Nord Krauskopf, and Rod Osterlund. He got four of his five career victories in 1975 and 1976 and was a consistent top-10 runner throughout the decade. His last victory came in 1982 at Richmond driving for himself. He's made more than 850 career starts, second only to Richard Petty's unreachable 1,177. What's more, he's done it with a limited budget that would have broken a lesser man.

A season filled with "Did Not Qualify" took a slight turn for the better when Dave Marcis started 32nd for the fifth annual Brickyard 400 at the Indianapolis Motor Speedway. He completed 102 of the 160 laps before the engine in his Chevrolet gave up, relegating him to 41st place.

Year	Car #	Sponsor	Make	SP	FP	Laps	Reason Out	Laps Led	Prize Money
1994	71	Terramite Equipment	Chevy	16	41	92	Accident	0	$21,825
1996	71	Prodigy	Chevy	40	35	112	Running	0	$50,185
1998	71	Realtree	Chevy	32	41	102	Engine	0	$67,635
Total						306		0	$139,635

Sterling Marlin, driver of the SABCO Racing Chevrolet, began his driving career almost by accident. His father, Clifton "Coo Coo" Marlin, was injured at Talladega in 1976 and needed a relief driver for his next race in Nashville, his home track.

Sterling crawled through the window of his father's car and brought it home in the top 10. Since that summer day, Marlin has known nothing but NASCAR racing. He went on to win the 1983 Rookie of the Year in NASCAR Winston Cup competition.

The Columbia, Tennessee, native has adapted well to such superspeedways as Daytona International and Talladega and has a total of six victories on those tracks. However, he's still searching for a win at Indianapolis Motor Speedway.

Two-time Daytona 500 winner (1994 and 1995) Sterling Marlin is the latest in a long line of drivers trying to find success with team owner Felix Sabates at Sabco Racing. He joined the No. 40 Chevrolet team after four years, two poles, and all six of his career victories with Morgan-McClure. Earlier in his career, the son of former driver Coo Coo Marlin ran a total of eight full Cup seasons for Roger Hamby, Billy Hagan, Junior Johnson, and the Stavola Brothers before going to Morgan-McClure.

Sterling Marlin started 11th and finished a lead-lap 11th for owner Felix Sabates in the 1998 Brickyard 400. It was his second-best Indianapolis Motor Speedway performance, ranking only behind his 7th place in 1995 with Morgan-McClure.

Year	Car #	Sponsor	Make	SP	FP	Laps	Reason Out	Laps Led	Prize Money
1994	4	Kodak Film	Chevy	9	14	160	Running	0	$49,000
1995	4	Kodak Film	Chevy	3	7	160	Running	15	$119,700
1996	4	Kodak Film	Chevy	11	39	37	Accident	1	$67,380
1997	4	Kodak Film	Chevy	13	43	2	Engine	0	$71,755
1998	40	Coors Light	Chevy	11	11	160	Running	0	$100,760
Total						519		16	$408,595

MARK MARTIN

Say the name Mark Martin and the word "contender" comes to mind. For Martin, the Brickyard 400 at the Indianapolis Motor Speedway has been a feast or famine affair.

In 1994, Martin had to endure disappointment. He started from the 10th position but struggled to get his Ford up to par. It was one of only three finishes he had out of the top 10 that year.

In 1995, Martin returned with a vengeance, starting from the 14th position and posting a 5th-place finish, his third of the season.

In 1996, Martin showed his ever-present strength again by starting the 160-lap event from the outside front row position and finishing a strong 4th.

A year later, Martin's qualifying effort wasn't quite as strong, because the team suffered chassis problems upon arriving at Indy. He rolled off the line in the 31st position but managed to log a 6th-place run by race's end.

Martin's car for 1998 was the best he had driven to that point. The new Ford Taurus carried silver paint which seemed to be a sign for success. He qualified 7th, and once he reached the top-five, he never left.

As the laps began to wind down, Martin made a charge through the field, getting as high as 2nd place behind eventual winner Jeff Gordon—then came the caution and the checkered flag. Martin's stout race car was capable of winning. He just simply ran out of time.

Mark Martin's perseverance has driven his rise toward the top of Winston Cup racing. A former four-time American Speed Association champion, he struggled in his first attempt at Winston Cup in the early 1980s. He left to run Busch races and regroup, then returned with Jack Roush in 1988. The rest is history. Following the 1998 season, Martin had earned 38 Cup poles, 29 Cup victories, 9 top-five point finishes, 5 IROC titles, almost $21 million in winnings, and 1989 Winston Cup Driver of the Year.

Mark Martin and Jack Roush make up one of the most formidable and determined teams in all of NASCAR racing. Except for a 35th-place finish in 1994, Martin and his No. 6 Valvoline Ford have gotten along well with the Indianapolis Motor Speedway.

Year	Car #	Sponsor	Make	SP	FP	Laps	Reason Out	Laps Led	Prize Money
1994	6	Valvoline/Reese's	Ford	10	35	140	Running	0	$34,300
1995	6	Valvoline	Ford	14	5	160	Running	0	$144,850
1996	6	Valvoline	Ford	2	4	160	Running	19	$195,235
1997	6	Valvoline	Ford	31	6	160	Running	0	$125,960
1998	6	Valvoline	Ford	7	2	160	Running	2	$248,375
Total						780		21	$748,720

Rick Mast saw his first stock car race when he was 10 years of age and was immediately hooked on the idea of becoming a driver. At age 12, he would sneak the family car, a 1965 Mercury Comet, out of the garage when his parents weren't home and race it down the dirt roads near Lexington, Virginia. Mast's ultimate goal was to be the next Richard Petty or David Pearson.

To make that thought become reality, he had to do some early wheeling and dealing, trading a cow for a race car. He needed the race car and the other party needed the cow, so it seemed like a fair enough swap. At age 16, he was on his way.

Short track competition was followed by a ride in the NASCAR Busch Series where he was a fixture for several years. In 1988, he finally got a chance at NASCAR Winston Cup racing with one of his heroes, former driver Buddy Baker.

In 1989, Mast very nearly won the Daytona 500 in an unsponsored car owned by Travis Carter. Many, including Rick himself, feel he would have won the race if he had not made a fuel stop.

A few other rides followed, but in 1991, Mast was hired by team owner Richard Jackson, and the two showed promise. They seemed to be really good at winning pole positions, earning one in 1992, 1994, and again in 1995.

Yes, it's true. Rick Mast sold a cow to buy his first race car. Born and reared in the historic Blue Ridge Mountains of Virginia, he got to Winston Cup after years of dirt-track racing and many more in the Busch Series. He came to full-schedule Winston Cup racing in 1991 with Richard Jackson, then went to Butch Mock for the 1997 season. He's been part of pole trivia twice: he started No. 1 for Richard Petty's last race in 1992 and was on the pole (and led the first two laps) at the inaugural Brickyard 400 in 1994.

Rick Mast took a NASCAR provisional to start the 1998 Brickyard 400.

Year	Car #	Sponsor	Make	SP	FP	Laps	Reason Out	Laps Led	Prize Money
1994	1	Bog Foot/Skoal Racing	Ford	1	22	159	Running	2	$103,200
1995	1	Skoal Racing	Ford	9	8	160	Running	0	$100,700
1996	1	Hooters	Pontiac	8	9	160	Running	0	$99,485
1997	75	Remington Arms	Ford	17	23	160	Running	0	$74,335
1998	75	Remington Arms	Ford	42	22	160	Running	0	$81,310
Total						799		2	$459,030

JEREMY MAYFIELD

Of all the young faces who have attempted to find their place in NASCAR during 1998, Jeremy Mayfield, driver of the Penske-Kranefuss Racing Ford, leads the list (and the points standings, for a good part of the season).

The 29-year old native of Owensboro, Kentucky, finally quenched his desire to win a NASCAR Winston Cup race in June of 1998 at Pocono. However, since winning, he suffered a string of poor finishes out of the top 15.

His visits to the Brickyard have been a growing experience.

In 1994, Mayfield qualified 31st in the Cale Yarborough Motorsports Ford and improved his position to 26th, two laps off the pace.

The following year, Mayfield improved greatly by qualifying in 8th but dropped two laps off the pace and finished 29th in the 41-car field.

In 1996, Mayfield found enough speed to take the 19th starting spot, but fell a lap off of the leaders and finished 25th.

Mayfield's best year to date came with team owners Michael Kranefuss and Carl Haas in 1997. He started the event from a respectable 16th-place and put together a solid assault on the leaders, finishing 5th.

Then came 1998, the year some predicted Mayfield to be the winner. He took his stout Ford, prepared by crew chief Paul Andrews, to the front after posting a qualifying position that matched his team number—12. But his day would end on Lap 67 after crashing hard into the first turn wall.

Jeremy Mayfield is the latest in a long line of drivers from Owensboro, Kentucky. The racing Waltrips came from there, as did the Green brothers, and a handful of Winston Cup and Busch Series crew chiefs. He came up through the go-kart, dirt-track, Late Model, and ARCA ranks, arriving at Winston Cup in 1993. He drove part of three seasons for Cale Yarborough Motorsports before an even swap sent him to Michael Kranefuss (later Kranefuss/Penske Racing) in exchange for John Andretti. His first Cup pole came at Talladega in July 1996 and his first victory at Pocono in June 1998.

The Kranefuss/Penske No. 12 Ford started 12th in the 1998 Brickyard 400 and was a solid contender until crashing alone in Turn 1 after just 67 laps. Jeremy Mayfield's 42nd-place finish was in marked contrast to 1997 when he was a lead-lap 5th place.

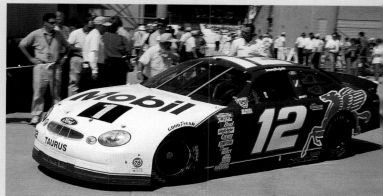

Year	Car #	Sponsor	Make	SP	FP	Laps	Reason Out	Laps Led	Prize Money
1994	98	Fingerhut	Ford	31	26	158	Running	0	$29,100
1995	98	RCA	Ford	8	29	158	Running	0	$53,275
1996	98	RCA	Ford	19	25	159	Running	0	$59,160
1997	37	Kmart/RC Cola	Ford	16	5	160	Running	0	$142,445
1998	12	Mobil One	Ford	12	42	67	Handling	0	$74,630
Total						702		0	$358,610

TED MUSGRAVE

Ted Musgrave learned patience and perseverance on the short tracks in his native state of Wisconsin. There he was regarded as a tremendous threat to win every week on the ARTGO, Winston All Pro, and ASA (American Speed Association) circuits.

In 1987, Musgrave won Rookie of the Year honors in the ASA. He was tapped, in 1990, to drive the Winston Cup car designated for Rich Vogler, who was killed at Salem Speedway that summer.

Musgrave earned three pole positions in 1994, the first year of the Brickyard 400. At Indianapolis, he qualified 37th but rallied back to log a solid 13th-place finish in his first year for Roush.

In 1995, Musgrave started the 160-lap event in 19th but improved his finish by three positions to 16th, again on the lead lap. The next year, Musgrave stalled in 21st position, starting and finishing there, but completing the full 160 laps.

Musgrave suffered his worst year yet in 1997 by starting 22nd and falling to 33rd, five laps off the pace at the end. With Roush for his 1998 Brickyard 400 start, he qualified 38th and managed a 19th-place finish, again on the lead lap.

Ted Musgrave came to Winston Cup racing with an impressive record, but the promising driver will have to wait until after the 1998 season for his first Cup victory.

Ted Musgrave was into the final weeks of his four-plus-year association with Roush Racing when he started 38th and finished a lead-lap 19th in the 1998 Brickyard 400. Two weeks later he was replaced by Kevin LePage who had been sitting out since late June waiting for Roush to make the change everyone knew was coming.

Year	Car #	Sponsor	Make	SP	FP	Laps	Reason Out	Laps Led	Prize Money
1994	16	Family Channel	Ford	37	13	160	Running	2	$52,800
1995	16	Family Channel	Ford	19	16	160	Running	0	$71,800
1996	16	TFC/Primestar	Ford	21	21	160	Running	0	$70,260
1997	16	TFC/Primestar	Ford	22	33	155	Running	0	$63,660
1998	16	Primestar	Ford	38	19	160	Running	0	$90,910
Total						795		2	$349,430

JERRY NADEAU

Danbury, Connecticut's Jerry Nadeau made his presence known to NASCAR Winston Cup racing with his participation in five events in 1997, but he did not make his first appearance at the Brickyard 400 until 1998.

Working with team owner Richard Jackson in 1997, Nadeau got the attention of the racing fraternity by posting a 9th qualifying position at New Hampshire International Raceway against the likes of Jeff Gordon, Dale Earnhardt, and Dale Jarrett.

Prior experience came with eight victories and Rookie of the Year honors in the Skip Barber Pro Series at Sears Point, California, as well as nearly a dozen starts in the Busch Series. Nadeau gained other experience in the 12 Hours of Sebring Endurance race and some IMSA events.

In 1998, Nadeau began the year with team owners Bill Elliott and NFL quarterback Dan Marino but was released from the team on July 1. He entered the Brickyard 400 with team owner Harry Melling. He started his rookie appearance at Indianapolis Motor Speedway in 41st and finished 26th, one lap down from the leaders

Former sports car road racer Jerry Nadeau seems determined to succeed in stock car racing. He relocated from his native Connecticut to Georgia in 1997 to drive the second Ford Taurus from the shop of Bill Elliott and NFL great Dan Marino. He was in the No. 13 car until the midpoint of the 1998 season when he moved to the No. 9 Ford to replace the injured Lake Speed.

After using a owner-points provisional to start 41st in the 1998 Brickyard 400, Indianapolis Motor Speedway rookie Jerry Nadeau finished 26th, one lap behind winner Jeff Gordon.

Year	Car #	Sponsor	Make	SP	FP	Laps	Reason Out	Laps Led	Prize Money
1998	9	Cartoon Network	Ford	41	26	159	Running	0	$81,885

JOE NEMECHEK

Joe Nemechek knows all too well the feeling of winning and has done so since he was 13 years old. In 1976, the Naples, Florida, driver began participating in motocross competitions and scored more than 300 wins in a six-year span.

That success inspired him to turn to stock cars in late 1986. By 1989, he had won Rookie of the Year honors in three divisions and a track championship in 1989. In 1990, Nemechek began fielding his own NASCAR Busch Series cars and two years later won the series championship as well as Most Popular Driver honors.

Nemechek wasted no time getting to the NASCAR Winston Cup Series. He made his debut at New Hampshire International Raceway in 1993, where he caught the eye of team owners Larry McClure and Larry Hendrick.

In 1994, Nemechek took a Hendrick Motorsports Chevrolet to the Brickyard 400 where he started 30th and improved that by 10 positions to 20th place, one lap behind race winner Jeff Gordon.

Nemechek turned a few heads in 1995 with his 6th-place qualifying effort but found himself two laps off the pace at race's end in 27th.

Florida native Joe Nemechek came to Winston Cup after a sparkling career in motocross, short-track Late Models, and the Busch Series, where he was 1992 champion. He moved to Winston Cup on a part-time basis in 1993, ran the full 1994 season for owner Larry Hedrick, then owned and fielded his own Cup team in 1995 and 1996. When the financial burden grew too heavy prior to the 1997 season, he sold the team to Felix Sabates (but stayed on as driver). He was the Busch Series' Most Popular Driver in 1992 and 1993 and is among the most accessible and popular in Winston Cup racing.

With backing from Bell South Mobility, Chevrolet driver Joe Nemechek started 17th and finished a lead-lap 24th in the 1998 Brickyard 400. The highlight of his four previous appearances at the Indianapolis Motor Speedway was his No. 2 starting position for the 1997 race.

Year	Car #	Sponsor	Make	SP	FP	Laps	Reason Out	Laps Led	Prize Money
1994	41	Meineke Muffler	Chevy	30	20	159	Running	0	$36,650
1995	87	Burger King	Chevy	6	27	158	Running	0	$51,675
1996	87	Burger King	Chevy	6	27	159	Running	0	$63,935
1997	42	BellSouth	Chevy	2	32	156	Running	0	$67,910
1998	42	BellSouth	Chevy	17	24	160	Running	0	$85,110
Total						792		0	$305,280

STEVE PARK

After 148 days on the sidelines due to a serious accident suffered at Atlanta Motor Speedway in March, Steve Park, driver of the Dale Earnhardt, Inc. Chevrolet, used the 1998 Brickyard 400 to return to action. The Islip, New York, native's performance proved there was no more pain in his right thigh bone, which had been severely broken in a practice session crash.

Park started the 1998 season in the running for NASCAR Rookie of the Year, but the leg injury got in the way. Instead, he chose to stand aside and concentrate on getting better.

The 1998 Brickyard 400 was Park's first attempt at the famed 2.5-mile speedway. He started the event from the 25th starting position but cut a tire and crashed with 12 laps remaining. Prior to that unfortunate incident, Park had gotten as high as 4th in the running order. After the crash took place, Park's yellow and black machine was too badly damaged to be in contention for the win.

Few drivers looked forward to the 1998 Brickyard 400 more than Rookie of the Year candidate Steve Park. He missed the season's 15 previous Winston Cup races after suffering multiple serious injuries in a vicious practice crash two days before the PrimeStar 500 at the Atlanta Motor Speedway. Intense rehabilitation got him back on his feet—literally as well as emotionally—in time to return for the Indianapolis race.

In his first Brickyard 400—and his first race since February at Rockingham—Steve Park started 25th in the Pennzoil-backed Chevrolet owned by Dale and Teresa Earnhardt. He had a solid top-10 run going until a blown tire caused him to crash out in Turn 4 just 12 laps from a cinch lead-lap finish.

Year	Car #	Sponsor	Make	SP	FP	Laps	Reason Out	Laps Led	Prize Money
1998	1	Pennzoil	Chevy	25	35	148	Accident	0	$68,025

KYLE PETTY

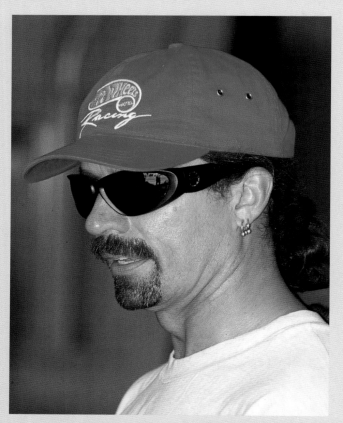

Of all the Pettys to compete in NASCAR Winston Cup competition, Kyle Petty is the only one to compete in the Brickyard 400. Grandfather Lee, father Richard, and uncle Maurice had all retired from driving or working as team mechanics when the Brickyard 400 came into existence in 1994.

Kyle Petty first drove for his family in 1979, beginning in ARCA competition (winning his first-ever race) and later joining the Winston Cup ranks. He teamed with the famed Wood Brothers of Stuart, Virginia, in 1985 and drove for team owner Felix Sabates from 1989 to 1996. Collectively, he scored eight career victories with those respective teams but elected to rejoin the family operation in 1997, forming pe2 (Petty Enterprises 2) that year.

The Brickyard 400 hasn't been very favorable to the Petty family.

In 1994, Kyle Petty started the race in 36th and improved 11 spots to 25th by race's end. He repeated this finish in 1995 after starting from the 32nd spot.

In 1996, Petty was involved in a hard crash on the front stretch on the 37th lap and suffered severe injuries that nearly sidelined him after qualifying an unlucky 13th. He came back the next year to post his best finish, this time a lucky 13th, after starting the race in 39th. For the first time in his Brickyard 400 career, he was able to complete all 160 laps.

In 1998, Petty scored a 14th-place finish after qualifying 33rd. Again, he was able to finish on the lead lap.

Kyle Petty became the first third-generation Winston Cup race winner in 1986 and has gone on to build a solid career with flair and charisma. He had full-season rides with his father's Petty Enterprises team, the Wood Brothers, and Sabco Racing before forming PE2 (Petty Enterprises 2) for the 1997 season. One of NASCAR racing's most generous and socially conscious personalities, he works tirelessly for charities inside and outside the sport. His annual motorcycle pilgrimage from California to North Carolina has raised hundreds of thousands of dollars for children's hospitals and youth-related charities from coast to coast.

After three consecutive poor finishes at the Indianapolis Motor Speedway—25th, 25th, and 38th—Kyle Petty seems to be figuring the place out. He finished a lead-lap 13th in the 1997 Brickyard 400 and was a lead-lap 14th in 1998.

Year	Car #	Sponsor	Make	SP	FP	Laps	Reason Out	Laps Led	Prize Money
1994	42	Mello Yellow/Kendall	Pontiac	36	25	159	Running	0	$39,000
1995	42	Coors Light	Pontiac	32	25	159	Running	0	$67,300
1996	42	Coors Light	Pontiac	13	38	37	Accident	1	$56,780
1997	44	Hot Wheels	Pontiac	39	13	160	Running	0	$78,035
1998	44	Hot Wheels	Pontiac	33	14	160	Running	0	$96,010
Total						675		1	$337,125

ROBERT PRESSLEY

The son of short track ace Bob Pressley, Robert Pressley (driver of the Jasper Motorsports Ford) grew up with the smell of rubber burning and the sound of loud engines screaming down the front stretch of a speedway. There was no question he would someday become a NASCAR driver; the only question was when.

In the early 1980s, Pressley, a native of Washington D.C., scored track championships at both New Asheville Speedway (North Carolina) and Greenville-Pickens Speedway (South Carolina). Pressley made his living on the short tracks of North Carolina and later in the NASCAR Busch Series before coming to the Winston Cup series in 1994 with team owner Leo Jackson.

In 1994, Pressley was not in the starting line-up for the first historic Brickyard 400 but did come back the next year to start 21st and finish 28th, two laps off the pace.

In 1996, Pressley started 34th but managed a 30th place finish, again three laps off the pace. Pressley once again missed the show in 1997, but captured the 20th starting spot in 1998 and finished 29th, three laps to the rear.

Just as his father before him in the 1960s and 1970s, Robert Pressley was a short-track terror throughout the 1980s in North and South Carolina. But Bob Pressley never moved to Winston Cup, leaving that honor to Robert, his driving son, and Charlie, his crew chief son. Robert was a successful Busch Series driver, winning nine times before going full-schedule Cup racing for the first time in 1995 with owner Richard Jackson. He ran only a handful of races in 1997 but signed in the off-season to run the full 1998 schedule for Doug Bawel and the Jasper Engines No. 77 Ford team.

It's amazing how similar Robert Pressley's 1997 and 1998 Brickyard 400s turned out to be. In 1997, he crashed out with three laps remaining and finished 30th. A year later, he crashed out with three laps remaining and finished 29th.

Year	Car #	Sponsor	Make	SP	FP	Laps	Reason Out	Laps Led	Prize Money
1995	33	Skoal Bandit	Chevy	21	28	158	Running	0	$69,875
1996	33	Skoal Bandit	Chevy	34	30	157	Accident	0	$58,935
1998	77	Jasper Engines & Trans	Ford	20	29	157	Accident	2	$84,085
Total						472		2	$212,895

JEFF PURVIS

12

As one of the greatest dirt track drivers in the country, Jeff Purvis will race anything on wheels. His only requirement is speed, and the Indianapolis Motor Speedway supplies plenty of that.

During the inaugural running of the Brickyard 400 in 1994, Purvis replaced Neil Bonnett, who lost his life in February of that year during a practice session crash at Daytona International Speedway. Purvis and team owner James Finch ran a select schedule that year that returned a few promising performances.

At the 1994 Brickyard, Purvis qualified the team's Chevrolet in 29th and finished 34th after completing 142 laps. He did not return to Winston Cup action until 1997. That year, he started the Brickyard race in 28th and finished in 37th after completing only 112 of the race's 160 laps.

Purvis became a regular in the NASCAR Busch Series, where he scored two victories

Ex-dirt tracker Jeff Purvis took the driver's seat in several Brickyard 400s.

In 1997, Purvis drove the No. 12 Opryland USA-sponsored car.

Year	Car #	Sponsor	Make	SP	FP	Laps	Reason Out	Laps Led	Prize Money
1994	51	Country Time	Chevy	29	34	142	Running	0	$22,500
1997	12	Opryland USA	Chevy	28	37	112	Running	0	$55,876
Total						254		0	$78,376

Ricky Rudd, driver of his own Fords at Rudd Performance Motorsports, is a master at keeping a winning streak alive. He's won at least one race per season for the past 16 seasons, a claim no other driver on the NASCAR Winston Cup circuit can make.

With over 600 career starts to his credit since he first joined NASCAR in 1975, he has 19 total career wins, one of which came at Indianapolis Motor Speedway.

Rudd was in his first year as a team owner in 1994. He qualified his Ford a strong 8th and finished 11th on the lead lap, not far away from Jeff Gordon's winning Chevrolet. Team ownership was agreeing with him.

In 1995, Rudd started the 160-lap event in 22nd but could only manage a 20th-place finish, one lap off the pace.

In 1996, Rudd struggled to qualify and had to settle for a 35th-place starting spot on the grid. But what a difference a race makes, as the Chesapeake, Virginia, native finished a strong 6th within striking distance of the win.

The dream came true in 1997. Rudd elected to stay on the track during a late-race caution and took his chances, winning the Brickyard 400 over Bobby Labonte. The win kept his winning streak alive for one more season.

In 1998, Rudd found himself near the front once again, giving everyone reason to think a second consecutive victory could be in the making, if leaders Gordon and Martin had problems. Unfortunately, Rudd crashed in the midst of a multi-car pile-up with two laps to go. He qualified 27th, but the wreck sent him back to 31st, five laps off the pace.

Ricky Rudd has enjoyed one of the most fulfilling careers of any NASCAR driver—even though he didn't have to work his way into Winston Cup from the lower NASCAR divisions. After an outstanding go-kart career, he was 17 when he jumped directly into Winston Cup in 1975 for the late Bill Champion. The 1977 Rookie of the Year had full-schedule rides with his family-owned team and with Donlavey Racing, DiGard Racing, Richard Childress Racing, Bud Moore Engineering, King Motorsports, and Hendrick Motorsports before creating his own RPM team (Rudd Performance Motorsports) in 1994. He was the 1992 IROC champion and has won at least one race for 16 consecutive seasons, including the 1997 Brickyard 400.

Ricky Rudd struggled in the 1998 Brickyard 400 but still was on the verge of a lead-lap, top-10 finish until getting swept up into a multi-car accident on a restart at Lap 155. He finished 31st, exactly 30 spots below where he finished in 1997.

Year	Car #	Sponsor	Make	SP	FP	Laps	Reason Out	Laps Led	Prize Money
1994	10	Tide	Ford	8	11	160	Running	0	$57,100
1995	10	Tide	Ford	22	20	159	Running	0	$73,450
1996	10	Tide	Ford	35	6	160	Running	1	$118,385
1997	10	Tide	Ford	7	1	160	Running	15	$571,000
1998	10	Tide/Whirlpool	Ford	27	31	155	Accident	0	$85,685
Total						794		16	$905,620

77

In 1981, Greg Sacks decided to leave the Modified cars of the Northeast to someone else and attempt to go NASCAR Winston Cup racing. He tested a car owned by former driver Richard Childress but was seriously injured in a crash at Daytona International Speedway. (Ironically, Sacks won his only NASCAR Winston Cup race at the same track four years later.)

Since 1983, the Mattituck, New York, native has been a fixture in NASCAR Winston Cup racing, driving for various team owners. He has entered the Brickyard 400 four times. In 1994, he wheeled a Jasper Motorsports Ford to 18th position after starting the race in 13th place.

Sacks joined team owner Dick Moroso at the Brickyard in 1995, qualifying 16th and finishing 33rd.

In 1996, Sacks drove for Gary Bechtel and started the race in 10th position. By race's end, he had fallen back to 32nd with a mechanical problem.

Sacks began the event in 37th in 1997 and improved to finish 31st.

Sacks elected to sit out the Brickyard in 1998 due to an injury suffered in April of that year.

A big-time stock car racer from Long Island? That's in New York, isn't it? It is, and Greg Sacks is the island's best-known motorsports professional. He came to Winston Cup in the mid-1980s, even while establishing an outstanding reputation in the rough-and-tumble Modified cars so popular in the Northeast. He's driven for 23 different owners but managed only two full seasons since 1983. His only career victory was the Pepsi Firecracker 400 at Daytona Beach in 1985. In it, he drive a tricked-up, unsponsored, plain-white No. 10 "Research and Development" Chevrolet for owner Bill Gardner and cagey crew chief Gary Nelson. Sacks began 1998 with the Cale Yarborough Motorsports team but was sidelined in April by major injuries suffered in a vicious crash at the Texas Motor Speedway.

Greg Sacks made his Indianapolis Motor Speedway debut in the 1994 Brickyard 400 in a Ford Thunderbird sponsored by Jasper Engines and USAir. He started 13th and finished a lap-down 18th, considerably better than the 33rd-, 32nd-, and 31st- place finishes he recorded the next three years.

Year	Car #	Sponsor	Make	SP	FP	Laps	Reason Out	Laps Led	Prize Money
1994	77	Jasper Engines/USAir	Ford	13	18	159	Running	4	$39,300
1995	32	Fina/Lance	Chevy	16	33	157	Running	0	$48,425
1996	29	Cartoon Network	Chevy	10	32	154	Running	0	$57,935
1997	91	Kruse Int'l./LJ Racing	Chevy	37	31	158	Running	0	$57,410
Total						628		4	$203,070

ELTON SAWYER

Elton Sawyer has often dreamed of earning a long-term assignment driving in NASCAR Winston Cup competition. In 1995 and 1996, he logged a total of 29 starts but was unable to put a competitive package together.

Sawyer drove Fords owned by Junior Johnson and, like everyone, hoped the teaming would be a good one. There were several shortcomings, however, and they soon parted ways.

At the Brickyard 400 in 1995, Sawyer only completed 17 laps before breaking an engine valve spring. He started the race in 41st and finished in last place.

Of all the drivers to qualify for the Brickyard, Elton Sawyer bears the dubious distinction of having the shortest Brickyard 400 career, completing only 17 laps in the 1995 race.

The No. 27 Ford sponsored by Hooters blew its engine on Lap 17, ending the team's day.

Year	Car #	Sponsor	Make	SP	FP	Laps	Reason Out	Laps Led	Prize Money
1995	27	Hooters	Ford	41	41	17	Engine	0	$55,520

Ken Schrader, driver of the Andy Petree Racing Chevrolet, looks poised to win the Brickyard 400 someday. The timing just hasn't been right for the St. Louis, Missouri, native so far.

Schrader began racing in 1971 at Lakehill Speedway near his hometown and was soon crowned track champion. Since those early days, he has gained a reputation for driving virtually anything on wheels as long as it's fast.

Schrader began his NASCAR Winston Cup career in 1985 with team owner Junie Donlavey and won Winston Cup Rookie of the Year honors. In 1987, Schrader moved to Hendrick Motorsports for the next eight seasons. From 1988 to 1996, Schrader only scored four wins, prompting the team owner and driver to part company. In 1997, Andy Petree formed his team and quickly hired Schrader as his pilot.

Despite winning only four Winston Cup races since 1988, Ken Schrader remains one of NASCAR's most popular and recognizable drivers. That's because there's hardly a track anywhere in American where he hasn't competed sometime during his career. He began in USAC Midget, Silver Crown, Sprints, and Stock Cars in the early 1980s, then joined NASCAR in 1984 with some help from Ford Motor Company. He was 1985 Rookie of the Year with owner Junie Donlavey in 1985 (they were together three seasons) and won his first race at Talladega in 1988 with Rick Hendrick, his owner from 1988 through 1996. He's currently into his second season with team owner Andy Petree and the famous Skoal Bandit No. 33 Chevrolet team.

When Ken Schrader started 19th and finished a lead-lap 10th in the 1998 Brickyard 400, he maintained his record of having finished all 160 laps in each of the five NASCAR events at the Indianapolis Motor Speedway. He finished 7th in the inaugural race and 19th, 16th, and 11th in the next three.

Year	Car #	Sponsor	Make	SP	FP	Laps	Reason Out	Laps Led	Prize Money
1994	25	Kodiak	Chevy	23	7	160	Running	0	$77,400
1995	25	Budweiser	Chevy	10	19	160	Running	2	$69,200
1996	25	Budweiser	Chevy	4	16	160	Running	2	$77,440
1997	33	Skoal Bandit	Chevy	8	11	160	Running	0	$95,235
1998	33	Skoal	Chevy	19	10	160	Running	0	$119,835
Total						800		4	$439,110

MORGAN SHEPHERD

At 58 years of age, Morgan Shepherd, driver of the Joe Falk Racing Chevrolet, seems to have no limits when it comes to being competitive in a stock car. The Ferguson, North Carolina, native has been a fixture in NASCAR Winston Cup racing since 1970. He has four career Winston Cup victories to his credit, but those numbers simply do not accurately describe the competitive nature he possesses.

Shepherd's résumé lists him as driving for many teams during his three decades of racing, but his best success came with team owner Cliff Stewart in 1982 when he won at Martinsville, Virginia. He drove for Jack Beebe in 1986 and earned a win at Atlanta. Shepherd gained another win at Atlanta in 1993 with the Wood Brothers and again with the Stuart, Virginia-based team in 1995.

When it comes to the Brickyard 400, Shepherd always seems to shine.

In 1994, he qualified his Wood Brothers Ford in 11th position and finished 10th on the lead lap. The following year, he posted a 33rd-place qualifying effort but managed to score a 10th-place finish again and was poised for a possible victory.

With a 38th-place qualifying effort in 1996 it looked as if a long afternoon was in the making. But Shepherd was careful and aggressive, logging his best career finish yet at Indy with a 5th-place run.

In 1997, he wasn't on the starting grid but came back in 1998 to qualify 36th and finish 15th.

North Carolina native Morgan Shepherd has been around NASCAR since 1970 and shows no signs of retiring anytime soon. He spent most of the 1970s and 1980s running a limited schedule before doing the full 1981 schedule for four owners, including Mark Martin. His full-schedule owners during the rest of the 1980s and 1990s include the following: Ron Benfield, Kenny Bernstein, Rahmoc Racing, Bud Moore, the Wood Brothers, and Butch Mock Motorsports. The first of his four victories came in 1981 at Martinsville with Cliff Stewart, his second in 1986 with Jack Bebee near Atlanta, then in 1990 with Moore near Atlanta, and in 1993 with the Woods near Atlanta.

When owner Joe Falk lost Kevin LePage to Roush Racing in July, Falk recruited Morgan Shepherd to drive his unsponsored No. 91 Chevrolet in the 1998 Brickyard 400. After being a lead-lap 10th with the Wood Brothers in 1995 and 1996 and 5th with Butch Mock in 1997, Shepherd was a lead-lap 15th for Falk's team.

Year	Car #	Sponsor	Make	SP	FP	Laps	Reason Out	Laps Led	Prize Money
1994	21	Citgo Petroleum	Ford	11	10	160	Running	0	$67,350
1995	21	Citgo Petroleum	Ford	33	10	160	Running	0	$94,000
1996	75	Remington Arms	Ford	38	5	160	Running	0	$140,135
1998	91	Little Joe's Autos	Chevy	36	15	160	Running	0	$91,810
Total						640		0	$393,295

MIKE SKINNER

Mike Skinner, driver of the RCR Enterprises Chevrolet, has made his mark on NASCAR racing since 1994.

Before that year Skinner had driven sporadically in Winston Cup competition. Team owner Richard Childress was looking for a driver to wheel his new NASCAR Truck Series team and placed a call to the Susanville, California, native. Originally, Skinner was uninterested, but after some strong persuasion, he finally agreed. The result was his winning the inaugural NASCAR Truck Series championship in 1995.

Skinner didn't get to the Brickyard 400 until 1996, but his entry was under tough circumstances. Teammate Dale Earnhardt was involved in a serious accident at Talladega Superspeedway the week before, breaking his sternum and receiving other nagging injuries. Childress tapped Skinner to drive for Earnhardt. He brought the car home 15th after the team started 12th.

In 1997, Skinner was once again driving for Childress, this time in his own NASCAR Winston Cup ride. He started the Brickyard 400 from the 6th position and still managed a finish in 9th, on the lead lap.

In 1998, Skinner posted his best finish to date at Indianapolis Motor Speedway. He started the event in 16th but quickly established himself as a contender. By race's end, Skinner posted a 4th-place position, close to winning his first official NASCAR Winston Cup event. Skinner's lone victory so far came in the special non-points event at Suzuka, Japan, in November 1997.

Mike Skinner made the move to Winston Cup after two successful years in NASCAR's Craftsman Truck Series. Driving for Richard Childress Racing, he won eight races and the series firstinaugural championship in 1995, then won eight more races in 1996. He was 1997 Winston Cup Rookie of the Year in Childress' second Chevrolet Monte Carlo team, working closely with seven-time champion Dale Earnhardt. In 1997, Skinner became the first rookie to win the pole for both the Daytona 500 and the Pepsi Firecracker 400 at the Daytona International Speedway. He drove relief much of the 1996 Brickyard 400 for Earnhardt, who had been injured a week earlier in a spectacular accident at Talladega.

After running 142 of the 160 laps in relief of Dale Earnhardt in 1996, Mike Skinner got his own ride for the 1997 and 1998 races. He started 6th and finished 9th as a true rookie in 1997, then came back to start 16th and finish 4th in the 1998 race.

Year	Car #	Sponsor	Make	SP	FP	Laps	Reason Out	Laps Led	Prize Money
1997	31	Lowe's	Chevy	6	9	160	Running	8	$132,560
1998	31	Lowe's	Chevy	16	4	160	Running	0	$187,325
Total						320		8	$319,885

LAKE SPEED

When the 1998 Brickyard 400 entries rolled off the line, longtime NASCAR Winston Cup veteran driver Lake Speed wasn't in the line-up. Just before teams arrived in Indiana, Speed resigned from Melling Racing, citing two bad crashes he suffered that year as reasons. The Jackson, Mississippi, native has had more than enough hard licks in his racing career, and family simply means more to him than risking his life again.

During a driving career that has gone from go-kart racing to Winston Cup action, Speed has enjoyed success behind the windshield and behind the team owner's desk. Speed's one big win came in 1988 at Darlington Raceway.

As for the Brickyard, Speed has enjoyed some good runs there as well.

In 1994, Speed struggled to qualify and settled for the 41st starting spot, but he salvaged a 15th-place finish. The next year, Speed qualified 27th and dropped to 34th, three laps down by race's end.In 1996, Speed enjoyed his best qualifying effort, a 3rd, followed by a 13th-place finish. Speed started 27th in 1997, posting his career best finish at Indianapolis, a 12th.

As of publication time, Speed's racing future remains uncertain, with permanent retirement a possibility.

Like a handful of other Winston Cup drivers, Lake Speed came to NASCAR after a sparkling career in world championship-level go-kart racing. He made his stock car debut in 1980 and has run most of the races in the ensuing 18 years. His only victory came at Darlington in the spring of 1988 with his own underfinanced team. He began 1998 with long-time patron Harry Melling and the Cartoon Network, then stepped aside shortly after the midpoint of the season after a series of nagging injuries affected his performance.

Lake Speed came from 41st to finish a lead-lap 15th with owner Bud Moore and sponsor Ford Quality Care in the 1994 Brickyard 400. He drove in 1995 (finishing 34th), 1996 (13th), and 1997 (12th) for owner Harry Melling.

Year	Car #	Sponsor	Make	SP	FP	Laps	Reason Out	Laps Led	Prize Money
1994	15	Quality Care	Ford	41	15	160	Running	5	$52,350
1995	9	Spam	Ford	27	34	157	Running	0	$48,175
1996	9	Spam	Ford	3	13	160	Running	2	$82,360
1997	9	Melling Auto Parts	Ford	27	12	160	Running	0	$83.135
Total						637		7	$266,020

JIMMY SPENCER

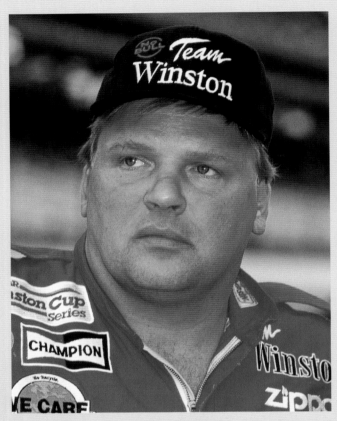

Jimmy Spencer is always a thrill to watch, no matter where he's racing or what he's racing in.

The Berwick, Pennsylvania, driver stormed the short tracks of the Keystone state with hundreds of wins, but his long-term goals centered on someday joining the NASCAR Winston Cup circuit. He got his wish in 1989, driving a limited schedule with team owner and driver Buddy Baker. Spencer would later drive for owners such as Rod Osterland, Travis Carter, and former drivers Bobby Allison and Junior Johnson.

It was with Johnson that Spencer broke into the Brickyard 400 line-up during NASCAR's first year at Indianapolis. In 1994, Spencer had already won races at Daytona and Talladega. In the Brickyard 400 he started 34th in Johnson's Ford but crashed on the 9th lap and finished 43rd. Spencer suffered a broken shoulder in the mishap.

Spencer joined Travis Carter for the full NASCAR Winston Cup schedule in 1995. At the Brickyard 400 Spencer put together a 38th-place qualifying run and finished in 23rd position.

In 1996, Spencer qualified 20th in Carter's yellow and purple Ford Thunderbird and finished 12th on the lead lap. The 1997 Brickyard 400 wasn't Spencer's best year. He had to settle for 40th starting position and finished in 24th, one lap behind the leaders.

Spencer had a good run going in 1998, starting from the 21st position. However, he cut a tire late in the race and finished 32nd, six laps behind winner Jeff Gordon.

No modern-day Winston Cup driver has a nickname as easily recognizable as Jimmy Spencer's. They call him "Mr. Excitement," an undeniable throwback to his days as one of NASCAR's most successful and exciting Modified tour drivers. After 1986 and 1987 Mod championships and Busch Series success, he graduated to NASCAR's top level in 1989. He drove for six different owners before landing with Junior Johnson in 1994, the year he won the mid-summer races at Daytona Beach and Talladega with McDonald's backing. When Johnson sold his team late that year, Spencer moved to the Camel- and Winston-backed team of owner Travis Carter.

Jimmy Spencer never has enjoyed much success at the Indianapolis Motor Speedway. He's never started better than 20th, and other than a 12th-place finish in 1996, has never come home better than 23rd. His 1994 appearance was with Junior Johnson, his next four starts (including his wreck-related 32nd place in 1998) with Travis Carter.

Year	Car #	Sponsor	Make	SP	FP	Laps	Reason Out	Laps Led	Prize Money
1994	27	McDonald's	Ford	34	43	9	Accident	0	$21,825
1995	23	Camel Cigarettes	Ford	38	23	159	Running	0	$59,200
1996	23	Camel Cigarettes	Ford	20	12	160	Running	0	$87,660
1997	23	Camel Cigarettes	Ford	40	24	159	Running	3	$74,435
1998	23	Winston Cigarettes	Ford	21	32	154	Accident	0	$78,285
Total						641		3	$321,405

HUT STRICKLIN

Following an impressive early racing career in the short track ranks, Hut Stricklin, a native of Alabama, finally got his first Winston Cup start in 1987.

Prior to his first start in the Brickyard 400 in its inaugural year, Stricklin drove for such prominent team owners as Rod Osterland, Rick Hendrick, Robert Yates, Junior Johnson, and Bobby Allison. At the start of the 1994 season, he joined team owner Travis Carter and qualified his Ford in 20th position but finished 36th after suffering a broken oil line.

In 1995, Stricklin joined Kenny Bernstein and started the 160-lap race in 29th. He managed a 22nd-place finish, one lap off the pace.

The following year, he joined Stavola Brothers Racing and qualified 16th, finishing two positions back in 18th on the lead lap.

Stricklin did not qualify for the event the next two seasons.

Hut Stricklin is among a handful of Winston Cup drivers to have come up through the ranks of NASCAR's subcompact Goody's Dash Series. He began on Alabama's short tracks in the late 1970s and kept coming through the Winston Racing Series, the All-American Challenge Series, and the Goody's Series, where he was 1986 champion. He's driven for 12 owners, among them Rod Osterlund, Rick Hendrick, Bobby Allison, Junie Donlavey, Junior Johnson, Larry Hendrick, Travis Carter, Kenny Bernstein, and the Stavola Brothers. He's still looking for his first career victory after almost 275 starts and his first top 10 in points after 10 full seasons.

After the Stavola Brothers closed down their No. 8 Circuit City Ford team midway through the 1998 season, Hut Stricklin was hired by Buz McCall to drive his No. 96 Caterpillar Chevrolet in several races, including the Brickyard 400. Stricklin was among the handful of drivers who didn't qualify.

Year	Car #	Sponsor	Make	SP	FP	Laps	Reason Out	Laps Led	Prize Money
1994	23	Camel Cigarettes	Ford	20	36	136	Oil Line	0	$24,000
1995	26	Quaker State	Ford	29	22	159	Running	0	$61,700
1996	8	Circuit City	Ford	16	18	160	Running	0	$66,560
Total						455		0	$152,260

Like A. J. Foyt, Danny Sullivan is an open-wheel racing legend who has won the Indianapolis 500. His victory in the 1985 race came after spinning his car in front of his closest challenger, Mario Andretti, while leading the race.

Sullivan entered the 1994 Brickyard 400 for two reasons—it was the first historic race at IMS involving stock cars and to jump-start his career, possibly with a Winston Cup ride. Driving a Chevrolet, he managed to qualify in the 26th position but could only muster a 33rd-place finish in the final rundown.

While Sullivan never made the leap to stock car racing, he was most certainly a part of the historic 1994 Brickyard 400.

Former Indianapolis 500 winner Danny Sullivan was one of only three drivers with Indy 500 experience (the others were A. J. Foyt and Geoff Brabham) to qualify for the inaugural Brickyard 400 in 1994. Sullivan won the 500 in 1985 with a famous "Spin and Win" move that still makes the Speedway's all-time highlight reel. The 1988 CART IndyCar Sseries champion has made a few NASCAR starts but never fared very well.

Danny Sullivan drove a No. 99 Chevrolet Lumina in the inaugural Brickyard 400 in 1994. The entry was owned by Chris Virtue, tuned by Fred Wanke, and sponsored by several Indianapolis-based businesses. Sullivan started 26th and finished 33rd but was running well until losing time in the pits while his crew installed a new left-rear window after the original piece blew out early in the race.

Year	Car #	Sponsor	Make	SP	FP	Laps	Reason Out	Laps Led	Prize Money
1994	99	Corporate Car of Indy	Chevy	26	33	152	Running	0	$22,750

Dick Trickle, driver of the Junie Dunlavey Ford, is another of those timeless wonders who seems to get better on the race track as years go by. The Wisconsin native has won more than 500 races in his 30-year career but is still looking for his first NASCAR Winston Cup victory after nearly 275 career starts.

Victory at the Indianapolis Motor Speedway still eludes him as well.

In 1994, Trickle went to the Brickyard 400 with team owner Dean Myers. That year, he was unable to make the starting line-up for the race.

However, Trickle came back the next year with team owner Bud Moore to start the event in 11th and finished just out of the top-15, in 18th place.

Trickle joined Donlavey for 1996, starting the team's Ford in 25th and improving the position by two to 23rd.

In 1997, Trickle once again failed to qualify for the Brickyard 400 but came back in 1998 to start 18th and finish in the same position.

The world may never know the precise number of Dick Trickle victories since many of his old haunts have long-since closed and the ones still open didn't always keep accurate records. Whether it's 750 feature wins or 900 or 1,200 doesn't matter to the hundreds of thousands of his fans. A Midwesterner by birth and Southerner by inclination, Trickle's free-wheeling lifestyle belies his 57 years and status as a doting grandfather. He came to NASCAR for the first time in the early 1970s, then returned in 1989 and was named Rookie of the Year. He's had full-schedule seasons with the Stavola Brothers, Cale Yarborough Motorsports, Bud Moore, and Junie Donlavey and had one-off or partial-season runs with 17 other teams.

Dick Trickle has completed all but one lap of the three Brickyard 400s he's run. The first was with Bud Moore and Quality Care in 1995, and the 1996 and 1998 races were with Junie Donlavey and his Heilig-Meyers sponsorship. Trickle was 18th with Moore and 23rd and 18th with Donlavey.

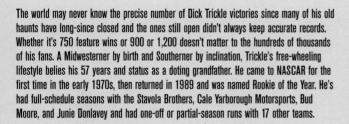

Year	Car #	Sponsor	Make	SP	FP	Laps	Reason Out	Laps Led	Prize Money
1995	15	Quality Care	Ford	11	18	160	Running	0	$69,500
1996	90	Heilig-Meyers	Ford	25	23	159	Running	0	$61,060
1998	90	Heilig-Meyers	Ford	18	18	160	Running	0	$91,610
Total						479		0	$222,170

Kenny Wallace, driver of the Fords owned by Filbert Martocci, followed his older brother Rusty into NASCAR Winston Cup racing. Like the careers of many others, there have been ups and downs.

Wallace spent part of his career in the NASCAR Busch Series before joining the Winston Cup ranks in 1990. After spending time with team owners Randy Hope, Sam McMahon, Felix Sabates, Charles Hardy, and Robert Yates, Wallace continues to search for his first NASCAR Winston Cup victory.

Wallace didn't start the Brickyard 400 until 1995 when he qualified 31st in a Martocci Ford and finished 37th, eight laps off the pace. His 1996 run saw him start from the 31st position and finish 33rd.

In 1997, Wallace started 29th and finished 30th, two laps off the pace. His 1998 performance saw him start the 160-lap event in 23rd, but engine problems on Lap 65 sent him to the sidelines.

What's a little brother to do? With Mike and Rusty already well-established racers, Kenny Wallace jumped in there and became a racer too. The Missouri native started in go-karts in the early 1980s, moved to the American Speed Association in 1986, and got to NASCAR's second-level Busch Series in 1989, when he was named Rookie of the Year. He ran a handful of Cup races in the early 1990s before going full-season for the first time with owner Felix Sabates in 1993. He ran a limited Cup schedule the next two years before joining Filbert Martocci for the 1996, 1997, and 1998 seasons. He still hasn't won but has two poles and has run well enough to show he's capable of winning like he did eight times during his Busch Series career.

Kenny Wallace started 23rd but was an early race, engine-related, 43rd-place DNF in the 1998 Brickyard 400. He wasn't in Winston Cup for the 1994 race, then finished 37th, 33rd, and 30th in the next three, all with team owner Filbert Martocci.

Year	Car #	Sponsor	Make	SP	FP	Laps	Reason Out	Laps Led	Prize Money
1995	81	TIC Financial	Ford	31	37	152	Running	0	$47,625
1996	81	Square D/TIC Financial	Ford	31	33	151	Engine	0	$50,865
1997	81	Square D	Ford	29	30	158	Running	0	$67,910
1998	81	Square D	Ford	23	43	65	Engine	0	$67,630
Total						526		0	$234,030

MIKE WALLACE

90

The brother of NASCAR Winston Cup regulars Rusty and Kenny Wallace, Mike Wallace has spent a few years of his racing career in the Winston Cup ranks. Despite winning races in virtually every form of stock car competition, he continues to search for that first Winston Cup win.

In 1995, Wallace made the Brickyard 400 field for team owner Junie Donlavey. He started the event from the 40th position and finished an impressive 26th. To date, it is his only Brickyard 400 start.

Presently, Wallace is out of the Winston Cup ranks and has turned his concentration to the NASCAR Craftsman Truck Series.

Despite his lack of Winston Cup success, Mike Wallace fills the family race shoes well. With solid success in the lower ranks, Wallace has moved on to a successful driving career in the Craftsman Truck Series.

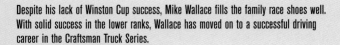

Mike Wallace was in the Junie Donlavey-owned, Heilig-Meyers-sponsored No. 90 Ford Thunderbird at the inaugural Brickyard 400 in August 1994. He made history by being the first driver on the track for the first day's first official practice session but wasn't nearly fast enough to make the field.

Year	Car #	Sponsor	Make	SP	FP	Laps	Reason Out	Laps Led	Prize Money
1995	90	Heilig-Meyers	Ford	40	26	158	Running	0	$55,975

When it comes to stock car racing, Rusty Wallace, driver of the Roger Penske-Don Miller Fords, has done just about all anyone can do to establish himself in the record books. Every time he straps himself into the car, he's a definite threat to win.

The St. Louis native is the son of a three-time track champion Russ Wallace and spent many hours around his dad's shop fantasizing about a driving career. A few short years later, all the dreaming and hard work began to pay off.

Wallace was USAC Rookie of the Year in 1979, ASA National Champion in 1983, NASCAR Winston Cup Rookie of the Year in 1984, NMPA Driver of the Year in 1988 and 1993, as well as the 1991 IROC champion. But his greatest thrill to date has been winning the 1989 NASCAR Winston Cup championship.

Winning the Brickyard 400 would certainly rank high on his achievement list, but he continues to search for that honor after coming very close.

When Rusty Wallace came charging out of the Midwest in the 1980s, almost everyone in NASCAR knew he'd be a star. After a handful of races with mediocre results, he went full-schedule racing in 1984 and 1985 with Cliff Stewart. He won 18 times with Raymond Beadle between 1986 and 1990 and garnered the 1989 Winston Cup by 12 points over Dale Earnhardt. He joined the potent Roger Penske team for the 1991 season and has added 29 more points-paying victories since then. He's won on every size NASCAR track except the super-fast ones at Daytona Beach and Talladega where almost everyone agrees it's only a matter of time.

The Penske-owned, Miller Brewing-backed No. 2 Ford has been among the most successful cars in the first five editions of the Brickyard 400. Rusty Wallace consistently finished well at the Brickyard.

Year	Car #	Sponsor	Make	SP	FP	Laps	Reason Out	Laps Led	Prize Money
1994	2	Miller Genuine Draft	Ford	12	4	160	Running	4	$140,600
1995	2	Miller Genuine Draft	Ford	24	2	160	Running	22	$250,500
1996	2	Miller Genuine Draft	Ford	17	7	160	Running	0	$112,985
1997	2	Miller Lite	Ford	43	38	91	Engine	0	$72,755
1998	2	Miller Lite	Ford	14	8	160	Running	0	$126,360
Total						731		26	$703,200

DARRELL WALTRIP

When Darrell Waltrip goes to the Indianapolis Motor Speedway, there is a certain chill that runs down his spine. It's a place that brings out great respect in all drivers, no matter what type of motorsport they participate in.

From an early age, Waltrip often listened to the Indianapolis 500 on the radio at his Owensboro, Kentucky, home. For weeks after each of those races, he would constantly dream of driving at the famed Brickyard. Turn by turn, he could hear the 350,000 people who fill the stands cheering for him. In his mind, he would drive an Indy car someday around the 2.5 miles of sacred pavement.

Waltrip was a three-time Winston Cup champion by the time he entered those gates in 1994 for the inaugural Brickyard 400, and his ride was a stock car, not an Indy car.

It's been quite a bumpy last few years for three-time NASCAR champion Darrell Waltrip. He's been stuck on 84 career victories since September of 1992, easily the longest losing streak of his brilliant 26-year career. He lost long-time sponsor Western Auto after 1997 and lost last-minute replacement Speedblock/Builders Square early into the 1998 season. Finally, he sold his No. 17 team to Texas businessman Tim Beverley and did a spring/summer stint as replacement driver (using his champion's provisional several times) for the injured Steve Park. Soon after Park came back, Beverly bought another Cup team and merged it with Waltrip's old outfit—although sponsorship concerns plagued the No. 35 Pontiac team into the fall. Regardless of all that, Waltrip's resume is truly outstanding: more than 750 career starts; 59 poles; 84 victories (including almost all the majors); more than $17 million in earnings; the 1981, 1982, and 1985 Winston Cups; and two Most Popular Driver awards.

After driving the No. 17 car in the first four Brickyard 400s, Waltrip spent the first part of 1998 driving the No. 1 Pennzoil car. In a deal inked only a few days before the Brickyard, Waltrip signed on to drive the No. 35 Tabasco Chevrolet in the race.

Year	Car #	Sponsor	Make	SP	FP	Laps	Reason Out	Laps Led	Prize Money
1994	17	Western Auto	Chevy	27	6	160	Running	0	$82,600
1995	17	Western Auto	Chevy	20	17	160	Running	0	$70,700
1996	17	Parts America	Chevy	33	40	9	Engine	0	$56,780
1997	17	Parts America	Chevy	4	14	160	Running	0	$85,085
1998	35	Tabasco Pepper Sauce	Chevy	43	13	160	Running	0	$89,610
Total						649		0	$384,775

With racing in his blood, there was little doubt that Michael Waltrip would eventually mix it up on the race track with his much older brother Darrell.

While Darrell was out winning NASCAR Winston Cup championships and establishing himself as a superstar, Michael busied himself racing go-karts near his Owensboro, Kentucky, home; this would lead to the much heavier street stocks later on.

From there, a natural progression took place. He became Kentucky Motor Speedway Mini-Modified champion 1981, NASCAR Dash champion in 1983, and finally made it to the NASCAR Winston Cup Series in 1985.

Like his brother, Michael often thought of running at the Indianapolis Motor Speedway but had no idea it would come in a stock car.

At the 1994 Brickyard 400, Waltrip drove the Bahari Racing Pontiac to an 8th-place finish after qualifying 15th. A year later, Waltrip started the race in 7th but finished on the lead lap in 14th place.

Waltrip joined forces with the famed Wood Brothers for 1996. He started the team's Ford in 30th and finished 28th. In 1997, he rolled off the line in 18th, bringing the car home 39th after completing only 89 of the scheduled 160 laps, due to involvement in a multi-car wreck.

In 1998, Waltrip (again driving the Wood Brothers Ford) struggled, qualifying 29th and improving that position by eight spots to 21st.

Michael Waltrip is bright, articulate, personable, and a sponsor's and sanctioning body's delight. But he hasn't won a points race in his 13 full seasons of Winston Cup and holds the dubious record for most career losses among active drivers who've never won even once. (Richard Petty lost far more than Waltrip ever will, but he also won a couple of hundred.) He began his Cup career with Dick Bahre in the mid-1980s, spent eight years with owners Chuck Rider and Lowrance Harry in the No. 30 Pontiacs, then spent 1996, 1997, and 1998 with the Wood Brothers. Waltrip won the 1996 Winston All-Star race near Charlotte for the Woods, but it doesn't count as an official event. Waltrip announced midway through 1998 that he wouldn't return to the Wood Brothers for a fourth season.

Michael Waltrip started 29th and finished a lead-lap 21st in the 1998 Brickyard 400. Instead of their traditional orange-and-white livery, the Wood Brothers and long-time sponsor Citgo unveiled a one-time-only blue design for the Indianapolis Motor Speedway event.

Year	Car #	Sponsor	Make	SP	FP	Laps	Reason Out	Laps Led	Prize Money
1994	30	Pennzoil	Pontiac	15	8	160	Running	0	$72,300
1995	30	Pennzoil	Pontiac	7	14	160	Running	1	$74,300
1996	21	Citgo Petroleum	Ford	30	28	159	Running	0	$62,435
1997	21	Citgo Petroleum	Ford	18	39	89	Running	0	$62,755
1998	21	Citgo Petroleum	Ford	29	21	160	Running	0	$93,410
Total						728		1	$365,200

RICK WILSON

27

From 1980 to 1997, Rick Wilson of Bartow, Florida, logged just over 200 starts in NASCAR Winston Cup competition without any victories to his credit. Included in this list of starts is the 1997 Brickyard 400.

Wilson began the 160-lap event from the 34th position in a Ford provided by a one-race sponsorship deal with the NFL's Indianapolis Colts football team. By race's end, Wilson managed a 21st-place finish on the lead lap.

Wilson continues to race on the local short track level hoping to find a competitive Winston Cup opportunity.

A 17-year Winston cup veteran, Rick Wilson's only Brickyard 400 appearance came in 1997.

Wilson's ride for 1997 was the No. 27 Ford sponsored by the Indianapolis Colts.

Year	Car #	Sponsor	Make	SP	FP	Laps	Reason Out	Laps Led	Prize Money
1997	27	Indianapolis Colts	Ford	34	21	160	Running	0	$65,935

OFFICIAL STARTING LINE-UP
Saturday, August 6, 1994

SP	#	Driver	Car Name	Team	Speed
1	1	Rick Mast	Big Foot/Skoal Racing Ford	Richard Jackson	172.414
2	3	Dale Earnhardt	GM Goodwrench Chevy	Richard Childress	171.726
3	24	Jeff Gordon	DuPont Chevy	Hendrick Motorsports, Inc.	171.125
4	7	Geoff Bodine	Exide Batteries Ford	Geoff Bodine Racing	170.982
5	22	Bobby Labonte	Maxwell House Pontiac	Bill Davis	170.794
6	11	Bill Elliott	Budweiser/Amoco Ford	Junior Johnson, Inc.	170.338
7	26	Brett Bodine	Quaker State Ford	Kenny Bernstein	170.084
8	10	Ricky Rudd	Tide Ford	Rudd Perf. Motorsports	169.933
9	4	Sterling Marlin	Kodak Chevy	Morgan McClure Racing	169.766
10	6	Mark Martin	Valvoline/Reese's Ford	Jack Roush	169.690
11	21	Morgan Shepherd	Citgo Petroleum Ford	Glen Wood	169.686
12	2	Rusty Wallace	Miller Genuine Draft Ford	Penske South Racing	169.683
13	77	Greg Sacks	USAir/Jasper Engines Ford	Jasper Motorsports	169.677
14	18	Dale Jarrett	Interstate Battery Chevy	Joe Gibbs	169.661
15	30	Michael Waltrip	Pennzoil Pontiac	C. G. Rider	169.587
16	71	Dave Marcis	Terramite Cst. Equip. Chevy	Marcis Auto Racing	169.514
17	28	Ernie Irvan	Texaco/Havoline Ford	Robert Yates	169.453
18	07	Geoff Brabham	Kmart Ford	Kranefuss-Haas Racing	169.310
19	9	Rich Bickle	Orkin Pest Control Ford	Harry Melling	169.214
20	23	Hut Stricklin	Camel Cigarettes Ford	Travis Carter	169.065
21	5	Terry Labonte	Kellogg's Chevy	Hendrick Motorsports	170.046
22	43	Wally Dallenbach Jr.	STP Pontiac	Richard Petty Enterprises	169.962
23	25	Ken Schrader	Kodiak Chevy	Joe Hendrick Motorsports	169.635
24	55	Jimmy Hensley	Bondo/Mar-Hyde Ford	Diane M. DeWitt	169.492
25	75	Todd Bodine	Factory Stores of Am. Ford	Butch Mock Motorsports	169.396
26	99	Danny Sullivan	Corporate Car of Indy Chevy	Chris Virtue	169.214
27	17	Darrell Waltrip	Western Auto Chevy	DarWal, Inc.	169.186
28	14	John Andretti	Bryant/Byrd's Chevy	Billy J. Hagan/Jonathan Byrd	169.182
29	51	Jeff Purvis	Country Time Chevy	James Finch	169.005
30	41	Joe Nemechek	Meineke Muffler Chevy	Larry Hedrick	168.989
31	98	Jeremy Mayfield	Fingerhut Ford	Cale Yarborough Motorsports	168.982
32	40	Bobby Hamilton	Kendall Oil Pontiac	Sabco Racing	168.966
33	31	Ward Burton	Hardee's Chevy	A. G. Dillard Motorsports	168.900
34	27	Jimmy Spencer	McDonald's Ford	Junior Johnson & Associates	168.890
35	44	Bobby Hillin	Buss Fuses Ford	Hardy Boys Motor Sports	168.789
36	42	Kyle Petty	Mello Yello Pontiac	Sabco Racing	168.742
37	16	Ted Musgrave	Family Channel Ford	Jack Roush	168.672
38	8	Jeff Burton	Raybestos Douglas Ford	William H. Stavola	168.672
39	02	Derrike Cope	Children's Miracle Net. Ford	T. W. Taylor	168.634
40	50	A. J. Foyt	Copenhagen Ford	AJ Foyt Enterprises	168.596
41	15	Lake Speed	Quality Care Ford	Bud Moore Engineering	Provisional
42	33	Harry Gant	Gas Am./Skoal Bandit Chevy	Leo E. Jackson	Provisional
43	58	Mike Chase	Tyson Foods Chevy	BMR Motorsports	

OFFICIAL STARTING LINE-UP
Saturday, August 5, 1995

SP	#	Driver	Car Name	Time	Speed
1	24	Jeff Gordon	DuPont Chevy	52.163	172.536
2	43	Bobby Hamilton	STP Pontiac	52.258	172.222
3	4	Sterling Marlin	Kodak Film Chevy	52.462	171.553
4	94	Bill Elliott	McDonald's Ford	52.506	171.409
5	18	Bobby Labonte	Interstate Batteries Chevy	52.560	171.233
6	87	Joe Nemechek	Burger King Chevy	52.589	171.138
7	30	Michael Waltrip	Pennzoil Pontiac	52.616	171.051
8	98	Jeremy Mayfield	RCA Ford	52.628	171.012
9	1	Rick Mast	Skoal Racing Ford	52.641	170.969
10	25	Ken Schrader	Budweiser Chevy	52.645	170.956
11	15	Dick Trickle	Quality Care Ford	52.649	170.943
12	11	Brett Bodine	Lowe's Ford	52.682	170.836
13	3	Dale Earnhardt	GM Goodwrench Service Chevy	52.701	170.775
14	6	Mark Martin	Valvoline Ford	52.712	170.739
15	5	Terry Labonte	Kellogg's Chevy	52.713	170.736
16	32	Greg Sacks	FINA/Lance Chevy	52.726	170.694
17	77	Bobby Hillin	Jasper Engines/USAir Ford	52.757	170.593
18	8	Jeff Burton	Raybestos Ford	52.798	170.461
19	16	Ted Musgrave	Family Channel Ford	52.820	170.390
20	17	Darrell Waltrip	Western Auto Chevy	52.823	170.380
21	33	Robert Pressley	Skoal Bandit Chevy	52.856	170.274
22	10	Ricky Rudd	Tide Ford	52.864	170.248
23	37	John Andretti	Kmart/Little Caesars Ford	52.887	170.174
24	2	Rusty Wallace	Miller Genuine Draft Ford	52.925	170.052
25	7	Geoff Bodine	Exide Batteries Ford	52.952	169.965
26	28	Dale Jarrett	Texaco/Havoline Ford	52.986	169.856
27	9	Lake Speed	Spam Ford	53.035	169.699
28	41	Ricky Craven	Kodiak Chevy	53.038	169.690
29	26	Hut Stricklin	Quaker State Ford	53.104	169.479
30	31	Ward Burton	Hardee's Chevy	53.116	169.440
31	81	Kenny Wallace	T. I. C. Financial Systems Ford	53.123	169.418
32	42	Kyle Petty	Coors Light Pontiac	53.217	169.119
33	21	Morgan Shepherd	Citgo Ford	53.256	168.995
34	75	Todd Bodine	Factory Stores of America Ford	53.260	168.982
35	22	Jimmy Hensley	MBNA America Pontiac	53.458	168.356
36	40	Rich Bickle	Kendall Pontiac	53.460	168.350
37	12	Derrike Cope	Straight Arrow Ford	53.473	168.309
38	23	Jimmy Spencer	Camel Cigarettes Ford	53.526	168.143
39	29	Steve Grissom	Meineke Chevy	Provisional	
40	90	Mike Wallace	Heilig-Meyers Ford	Provisional	
41	27	Elton Sawyer	Hooter's Ford	Provisional	

Note: Positions 1–20 were determined by qualification on Thursday, August 3. Because of a complete rain-out on Friday, August 4, positions 21–38 were determined using qualification times from Thursday also. Positions 39–41 were filled according to NASCAR provisional starter rules.

OFFICIAL STARTING LINE-UP
Saturday, August 3, 1996

SP	#	Driver	Car Name	Time	Speed
1	24	Jeff Gordon	DuPont Chevy	51.015	176.419*
2	6	Mark Martin	Valvoline Ford	51.159	175.922
3	9	Lake Speed	Spam Ford	51.183	175.840
4	25	Ken Schrader	Budweiser Chevy	51.298	175.445
5	77	Bobby Hillin	Jasper Engines/F-M Ford	51.328	175.343
6	87	Joe Nemechek	Burger King Chevy	51.331	175.333
7	94	Bill Elliott	McDonald's Ford	51.390	175.131
8	1	Rick Mast	Hooter's Pontiac	51.406	175.077
9	5	Terry Labonte	Kellogg's Chevy	51.413	175.053
10	29	Greg Sacks	Cartoon Network Chevy	51.439	174.965
11	4	Sterlin Marlin	Kodak Film Chevy	51.443	174.951
12	3	Dale Earnhardt	GM Goodwrench Chevy	51.455	174.910
13	42	Kyle Petty	Coors Light Pontiac	51.455	174.910
14	30	Johnny Benson	Pennzoil Pontiac	51.465	174.876
15	28	Ernie Irvan	Texaco Havoline Ford	51.502	174.750
16	8	Hut Stricklin	Circuit City Ford	51.513	174.713
17	2	Rusty Wallace	Miller Ford	51.515	174.706
18	15	Wally Dallenbach, Jr.	Hayes Modems Ford	51.589	174.456
19	98	Jeremy Mayfield	RCA Ford	51.592	174.446
20	23	Jimmy Spencer	Camel Cigarettes Ford	51.597	174.429
21	16	Ted Musgrave	Fam. Chan./Prmstr. Ford	51.600	174.419
22	11	Brett Bodine	Lowe's Ford	51.607	174.395
23	18	Bobby Labonte	Interstate Batteries Chevy	51.628	174.324
24	88	Dale Jarrett	Quality Care Ford	51.647	174.260
25	90	Dick Trickle	Heilig-Meyers Ford	51.664	174.203
26	95	Gary Bradberry	Shoney's Restaurant Ford	51.551	174.584
27	37	John Andretti	Kmart/Little Caesars Ford	51.676	174.162
28	99	Jeff Burton	Exide Batteries Ford	51.715	174.031
29	7	Geoff Bodine	QVC Ford	51.785	173.796
30	21	Michael Waltrip	Citgo Ford	51.873	173.501
31	81	Kenny Wallace	Square D/TIC Ford	51.877	173.487
32	22	Ward Burton	MBNA America Pontiac	51.941	173.274
33	17	Darrell Waltrip	Parts America Chevy	51.960	173.210
34	33	Robert Pressley	Skoal Bandit Chevy	51.971	173.174
35	10	Ricky Rudd	Tide Ford	51.977	173.154
36	12	Derrike Cope	Badcock Ford	51.977	173.154
37	43	Bobby Hamilton	STP Pontiac	52.037	172.954
38	75	Morgan Shepherd	Remington Arms Ford	52.045	172.927
39	41	Ricky Craven	Kodiak Chevy	Provisional	
40	71	Dave Marcis	Prodigy Chevy	Provisional	

* New Track Record

OFFICIAL STARTING LINE-UP
Saturday, August 2, 1997

SP	#	Driver	Car Name	Team	Speed
1	28	Ernie Irvan	Texaco Havoline Ford	Robert Yates	*177.736
2	42	Joe Nemechek	BellSouth Chevy	Felix Sabates	177.550
3	88	Dale Jarrett (W)	Quality Care/Ford Credit Ford	Robert Yates	177.494
4	17	Darrell Waltrip	Parts America Chevy	Darrell Waltrip	176.866
5	3	Dale Earnhardt (W)	GM Goodwrench Chevy	Richard Childress	176.536
6	31	Mike Skinner (#R)	Lowe's Chevy	Richard Childress	176.415
7	10	Ricky Rudd	Tide Ford	Ricky Rudd	176.184
8	33	Ken Schrader	Skoal Chevy	Andy Petree	176.170
9	96	David Green (#R)	Caterpillar Chevy	Howard McCall	176.149
10	26	Rich Bickle	KFC Team Twister Chevy	Darrell Waltrip	176.087
11	40	Robby Gordon (#R)	Coors Light Chevy	Felix Sabates	176.074
12	43	Bobby Hamilton	STP Pontiac	Richard Petty	176.053
13	4	Sterling Marlin	Kodak Film Chevy	Larry McClure	175.977
14	46	Wally Dallenbach, Jr.	First Union Chevy	Carolyn Sabates	175.884
15	94	Bill Elliott	McDonald's Ford	Bill Elliott	175.833
16	37	Jeremy Mayfield	Kmart/RC Cola Ford	Michael Kranefuss/Carl Haas	175.812
17	75	Rick Mast	Remington Arms Ford	Butch Mock	175.709
18	21	Michael Waltrip	Citgo Ford	Glen Wood	175.671
19	41	Steve Grissom	Kodiak Chevy	Larry Hedrick	175.415
20	30	Johnny Benson, Jr.	Pennzoil Pontiac	C.G. Rider/Lowrance Harry	175.223
21	97	Chad Little (#)	John Deere Pontiac	Greg Pollex	175.145
22	16	Ted Musgrave	Family Channel/Primestar Ford	Jack Roush	175.128
23	92	Ron Barfield, Jr. (#)	New Holland Ford	Bill Elliott	175.087
24	24	Jeff Gordon (W)	DuPont Refinishes Chevy	Rick Hendrick	175.056
25	18	Bobby Labonte	Interstate Batteries Pontiac	Joe Gibbs	175.043
26	29	Jeff Green (#R)	Cartoon Network Chevy	Gary Bechtel	176.153
27	9	Lake Speed	Melling Engine Parts Ford	Harry S. Melling	175.210
28	12	Jeff Purvis	Opryland USA Chevy	Dennis Adcock	175.169
29	81	Kenny Wallace	Square D Ford	Filbert Martocci	175.097
30	95	Ed Berrier (#)	Shoney's Inn Chevy	Earl Sadler	175.012
31	6	Mark Martin	Valvoline Ford	Jack Roush	174.917
32	36	Derrike Cope	Skittles Pontiac	Nelson Bowers II	174.900
33	99	Jeff Burton	Exide Batteries Ford	Jack Roush	174.869
34	27	Rick Wilson (#)	Blair Motorsports Ford	David Blair	174.832
35	98	John Andretti	RCA Ford	Cale Yarborough	174.791
36	22	Ward Burton	MBNA America Pontiac	Bill Davis	174.757
37	91	Greg Sacks	LJ Racing Chevy	Joseph A. Falk/LJ Racing	174.689
38	5	Terry Labonte	Kellogg's Chevy	Rick Hendrick	174.635
39	44	Kyle Petty	Hot Wheels Pontiac	Kyle Petty/David N. Evans	Provisional
40	23	Jimmy Spencer	Camel Ford	Travis Carter	Provisional
41	25	Ricky Craven	Budweiser Chevy	Rick Hendrick	Provisional
42	11	Brett Bodine	Close Call Ford	Brett Bodine	Provisional
43	2	Rusty Wallace	Miller Lite Ford	Roger Penske	Provisional

* New track record

123

1998 BRICKYARD 400 ENTRY LIST

Car	Yr.	Driver/Hometown	Sponsor	Make	Team	Owner
00	0	Buckshot Jones/Tucker, GA	Real Tree	Chevy	Stavola Brothers	William Stavola
01	0	Steve Park/East Northport, NY	Pennzoil	Chevy	Dale Earnhardt, Inc.	Teresa Earnhardt
2	4	Rusty Wallace/St. Louis, MO	Miller Lite	Ford	Penske South Racing	Donald J. Miller
3	4	Dale Earnhardt/Kannapolis, NC	GM Goodwrench Service Plus	Chevy	Richard Childress Racing	Richard Childress
4	4	Bobby Hamilton/Nashville, TN	Kodak Film	Chevy	Morgan-McClure Motorsports	Larry McClure
5	4	Terry Labonte/Corpus Christi, TX	Kellogg's/Quaker State/ Starburst/GMAC	Chevy	Hendrick Motorsports	Rick Hendrick
6	4	Mark Martin/Batesville, AR	Valvoline	Ford	Roush Racing	Jack Roush
07	0	Dan Pardus/Daytona Beach, FL	Midwest Transit	Chevy	Midwest Transit Racing	Hal Hicks/Mike Witters
7	4	Geoff Bodine/Chemung, NY	Philips Consumer Communications	Ford	Mattei Motorsports	Jim Mattei
9	0	Jerry Nadeau/Danbury, CT	Cartoon Network/ Melling Engine Parts	Ford	Melling Racing	Harry Melling
10	4	Ricky Rudd/Chesapeake, VA	Tide/Whirlpool	Ford	Rudd Performance Motorsports	Ricky Rudd
11	4	Brett Bodine/Chemung, NY	Paychex	Ford	Scandia/Bodine Motorsports	Brett Bodine/Andy Evans
12	4	Jeremy Mayfield/Owensboro, KY	Mobil 1	Ford	Penske-Kranefuss Racing	R. Penske/M. Kranefuss
13	NA	Wally Dallenbach Jr./NA	First Plus Financial	Ford	Elliott-Marino Motorsports	Bill Elliott/Dan Marino
14	NA	NA	NA	Pontiac	Richard Jackson Motorsports	Richard D. Jackson
15	0	Tim Steele/Grand Rapids, MI	Rescue	Ford	Robinson/Moore Motorsports	Bud Moore
16	4	Ted Musgrave/Evanston, IL	Primestar	Ford	Roush Racing	Jack Roush
17	4	Darrell Waltrip/Franklin, TN	Universal Studios/ American Graffiti	Chevy	Tyler Motorsports	Tim Beverley
18	4	Bobby Labonte/Corpus Christi, TX	Interstate Batteries	Pontiac	Joe Gibbs Racing	Joe Gibbs
19	1	Robby Gordon/Orange, CA	Yellow Freight	Ford	Roehrig Motorsports	Kurt Roehrig
21	4	Michael Waltrip/Owensboro, KY	CITGO Petroleum Corporation	Ford	Wood Brothers Racing	Glen Wood
22	4	Ward Burton/South Boston, VA	MBNA America	Pontiac	Bill Davis Racing	Bill Davis
23	4	Jimmy Spencer/Berwick, PA	Winston Cigarettes	Ford	Travis Carter Enterprises	Travis Carter
24	4	Jeff Gordon/Pittsboro, IN	DuPont/Quaker State/ Pepsi/GMAC	Chevy	Hendrick Motorsports	Rick Hendrick

No.		Driver/Hometown	Sponsor	Make	Team	Owner
26	2	Johnny Benson Jr./Grand Rapids, MI	Cheerios	Ford	Roush Racing	Evan Lyall
28	0	Kenny Irwin Jr./Indianapolis, IN	Texaco/Havoline	Ford	Robert Yates Racing	Robert Yates
30	4	Derrike Cope/Spanaway, WA	Gumout	Pontiac	Bahari Racing	Chuck Rider
31	1	Mike Skinner/Ontario, CA	Lowe's	Chevy	Richard Childress Racing	Richard Childress
33	4	Ken Schrader/Fenton, MO	Skoal	Chevy	Skoal Bandit Racing	Andy Petree
35	3	Wally Dallenbach Jr./Basalt, CO	Tabasco Brand Pepper Sauce	Pontiac	ISM Racing	L. G. "Bob" Hancher Jr.
36	3	Ernie Irvan/Salinas, CA	Skittles	Pontiac	MB2 Motorsports	C. Read Morton Jr.
40	4	Sterling Marlin/Columbia, TN	Coors Light	Chevy	Team SABCO	Felix Sabates
41	2	Steve Grissom/Gadsden, AL	Kodiak	Chevy	Larry Hedrick Motorsports	Larry Hedrick
42	4	Joe Nemechek/Lakeland, FL	BellSouth	Chevy	Team SABCO	Felix Sabates
43	4	John Andretti/Indianapolis, IN	STP	Pontiac	Petty Enterprises	Richard Petty
44	4	Kyle Petty/Randleman, NC	Hot Wheels	Pontiac	PE2	Kyle Petty
46	1	Jeff Green/Owensboro, KY	First Union	Chevy	Team SABCO	Carolyn Sabates
50	3	Ricky Craven/Newburgh, ME	Budweiser/Quaker State/Pedigree/GMAC	Chevy	Joe Hendrick Motorsports	Joe Hendrick
71	3	Dave Marcis/Wausau, WI	Realtree	Chevy	Marcis Auto Racing	Helen Marcis
75	4	Rick Mast/Rockbridge Baths, VA	Remington Arms	Ford	Butch Mock Motorsports	Butch Mock
77	2	Robert Pressley/Asheville, NC	Jasper Engines & Transmissions	Ford	Jasper Motorsports	Doug Bawel
78	2	Gary Bradberry/Chelsea, AL	Pilot Travel Centers	Ford	Triad Motorsports	Triad Motorsports
81	3	Kenny Wallace/St. Louis, MO	Square D	Ford	Filmar Racing	Filbert Martocci
88	4	Dale Jarrett/Conover, NC	Quality Care Service/Ford Credit	Ford	Robert Yates Racing	Robert Yates
90	3	Dick Trickle/Wisconsin Rapids, WI	Heilig-Meyers/Simmons	Ford	Donlavey Racing	W. C. Donlavey Jr.
91	NA	Morgan Shepherd/NA	Little Joe's Autos	Chevy	L. J. Racing, Inc.	Joseph Falk
92	0	Elliott Sadler/Emporia, VA	NA	Chevy	Diamond Ridge Motorsports	Gary Bechtel
94	4	Bill Elliott/Dawsonville, GA	McDonald's	Ford	Bill Elliott Racing	Bill Elliott
95	0	Andy Hillenburg/Indianapolis, IN	Shoney's Inn	Chevy	Sadler Racing	Earl Sadler
96	3	Hut Stricklin/Calera, AL	Caterpillar	Chevy	American Equipment Racing	Howard "Buz" McCall Jr.
97	1	Chad Little/Spokane, WA	John Deere	Ford	Roush Racing	Jack Roush
98	1	Rich Bickle/Edgerton, WI	Thorn Apple Valley	Ford	Yarborough Motorsports	Cale Yarborough
99	4	Jeff Burton/South Boston, VA	Exide Batteries	Ford	Roush Racing	Bob Corn

1998 BRICKYARD 400
Driver Position in 10-Lap Intervals

POS	Driver SP	SP	1	10	20	30	40	50	60	70	80	90	100	110	120	130	140	150	160	Driver FP	FP
1	Ernie Irvan	36	36	36	24	24	36	24	88	88	88	24	24	24	77	24	24	24	24	Jeff Gordon	24
2	Dale Jarrett	88	24	24	36	12	5	88	24	24	6	6	6	6	90	18	18	6	6	Mark Martin	6
3	Jeff Gordon	24	88	88	88	88	00	36	6	6	24	36	28	36	3	3	6	31	18	Bobby Labonte	18
4	Kenny Irwin Jr.	28	28	28	12	36	24	6	36	36	18	28	36	18	31	31	3	36	31	Mike Skinner	31
5	Jeff Green	46	50	18	28	2	88	2	2	1	5	5	18	28	40	6	31	3	3	Dale Earnhardt	3
6	Ricky Craven	50	46	12	6	28	3	5	28	18	28	18	5	5	24	5	5	43	36	Ernie Irvan	36
7	Mark Martin	6	18	6	2	43	28	28	1	28	3	40	3	3	18	36	36	5	43	John Andretti	43
8	Terry Labonte	5	6	43	43	6	22	1	5	5	40	3	1	1	5	10	10	2	2	Rusty Wallace	2
9	John Andretti	43	12	2	31	18	2	3	18	3	36	1	40	40	10	43	43	33	5	Terry Labonte	5
10	Bobby Labonte	18	43	46	33	46	6	18	3	40	31	90	31	90	36	2	2	40	33	Ken Schrader	33
11	Sterling Marlin	40	5	5	18	5	1	40	40	22	35	31	90	42	43	40	33	94	40	Sterling Marlin	40
12	Jeremy Mayfield	12	40	42	46	31	81	22	22	94	44	16	42	94	94	33	40	35	94	Bill Elliott	94
13	Geoff Bodine	7	2	7	22	3	18	00	81	42	50	94	94	16	6	23	94	90	35	Darrell Waltrip	35
14	Rusty Wallace	2	7	50	90	42	94	81	00	43	4	42	16	44	33	94	1	50	44	Kyle Petty	44
15	Buckshot Jones	00	31	40	5	94	40	94	94	91	97	44	44	2	23	1	35	44	91	Morgan Shepherd	91
16	Mike Skinner	31	42	33	13	22	31	31	42	90	26	35	35	10	1	35	44	23	88	Dale Jarrett	88
17	Joe Nemechek	42	00	31	00	40	50	42	12	16	21	4	91	43	35	44	23	91	50	Ricky Craven	50
18	Dick Trickle	90	90	00	3	90	16	50	31	31	43	91	2	91	2	50	50	18	90	Dick Trickle	90
19	Ken Schrader	33	33	99	42	00	26	16	91	44	42	75	10	35	44	46	90	46	16	Ted Musgrave	16
20	Robert Pressley	77	77	90	16	1	75	26	43	50	11	10	43	75	50	75	46	16	4	Bobby Hamilton	4
21	Jimmy Spencer	23	23	13	94	16	42	91	90	35	71	50	41	50	97	90	91	75	21	Michael Waltrip	21
22	W. Dallenbach Jr.	13	13	81	40	13	90	75	16	10	1	21	4	21	75	16	16	4	75	Rick Mast	75
23	Kenny Wallace	81	81	3	50	81	46	90	50	23	16	43	75	33	21	41	75	41	41	Steve Grissom	41

Pos	Driver	42 Joe Nemechek	26 J. Benson Jr.	9 Jerry Nadeau	00 Buckshot Jones	97 Chad Little	77 R. Pressley	46 Jeff Green	10 Ricky Rudd	23 Jimmy Spencer	11 Brett Bodine	22 Ward Burton	1 Steve Park	99 Jeff Burton	7 Geoff Bodine	28 K. Irwin Jr.	98 Rich Bickle	13 W. Dallenbach Jr	71 Dave Marcis	12 J. Mayfield	81 Kenny Wallace
24	Bobby Hamilton	4	1	23	10	10	41	46	26	26	10	41	50	23	91	97	21	97	97	97	42
25	Steve Park	1	10	81	50	81	77	41	44	75	23	97	46	91	41	41	41	21	41	41	26
26	Steve Grissom	41	3	1	91	91	23	23	75	4	90	77	23	46	46	97	75	4	75	21	9
27	Ricky Rudd	10	4	10	77	35	43	43	23	77	90	35	77	16	31	77	23	43	77	4	77
28	Dale Earnhardt	3	41	77	1	21	13	13	46	35	94	97	97	4	97	13	13	42	97	94	97
29	Michael Waltrip	21	22	44	21	41	44	10	10	13	13	77	2	88	42	77	44	77	26	13	26
30	Ward Burton	22	99	21	77	23	77	35	91	77	91	23	23	26	00	88	4	88	77	91	46
31	Rich Bickle	98	21	77	23	75	10	10	41	41	41	10	26	9	88	9	33	26	44	41	10
32	Dave Marcis	71	98	97	97	97	35	41	4	21	2	11	00	9	9	26	26	9	9	41	23
33	Kyle Petty	44	16	91	44	44	21	77	16	77	33	00	42	26	26	9	9	00	00	00	11
34	Jeff Burton	99	97	71	11	26	71	13	97	13	77	33	11	28	11	11	88	11	11	11	22
35	Chad Little	97	16	94	75	35	98	4	97	4	46	71	22	11	22	22	11	22	22	22	1
36	Morgan Shepherd	91	44	26	98	98	97	11	21	11	00	9	28	22	99	13	13	99	99	99	99
37	Bill Elliott	94	97	4	35	4	71	71	71	71	88	11	99	99	7	71	71	7	7	7	7
38	Ted Musgrave	16	94	98	9	9	98	98	11	9	9	22	7	13	13	22	22	13	28	28	28
39	Johnny Benson Jr.	26	11	11	11	11	9	9	9	9	22	81	22	71	7	13	13	13	13	13	98
40	Brett Bodine	11	26	75	26	33	33	33	33	98	99	99	99	7	7	99	98	71	71	71	13
41	Jerry Nadeau	9	75	35	71	71	12	12	98	98	98	98	81	98	98	98	98	98	98	98	71
42	Rick Mast	75	9	9	99	99	99	99	7	7	7	7	7	81	81	81	81	81	81	81	12
43	Darrell Waltrip	35	35	71	7	7	7	7	12	12	12	12	12	12	12	12	12	12	12	12	81
	Race Average Speed:	164	136	121	134	141	131	127	129	126	168	134	128	138	134	128	134	131	127	128	131

OFFICIAL STARTING LINE-UP
Saturday, August 1, 1998

SP	Car	Yr	Driver	Car Name	Time	Speed
1	36	3	Ernie Irvan	Skittles Pontiac	50.169	*179.394
2	88	4	Dale Jarrett	Quality Care Ford	50.393	178.596
3	24	4	Jeff Gordon	DuPont Chevy	50.470	178.324
4	28	0	Kenny Irwin Jr.	Texaco/Havoline Ford	50.488	178.260
5	46	1	Jeff Green	Money Store Chevy	50.586	177.915
6	50	3	Ricky Craven	Budweiser Chevy	50.647	177.701
7	6	4	Mark Martin	Valvoline Ford	50.679	177.588
8	5	4	Terry Labonte	Kellogg's Chevy	50.723	177.434
9	43	4	John Andretti	STP Pontiac	50.779	177.239
10	18	4	Bobby Labonte	Interstate Pontiac	50.867	176.932
11	40	4	Sterling Marlin	Coors Light Chevy	50.891	176.849
12	12	4	Jeremy Mayfield	Mobil 1 Ford	50.892	176.845
13	7	3	Geoff Bodine	Philips Comm. Ford	50.939	176.682
14	2	4	Rusty Wallace	Miller Lite Ford	50.944	176.665
15	00	0	Buckshot Jones	Real Tree Extra Chevy	50.988	176.512
16	31	1	Mike Skinner	Lowe's Chevy	50.995	176.488
17	42	4	Joe Nemechek	BellSouth Chevy	51.027	176.377
18	90	3	Dick Trickle	Heilig-Meyers Ford	51.057	176.274
19	33	4	Ken Schrader	Skoal Chevy	51.066	176.243
20	77	2	Robert Pressley	Jasper Engines Ford	51.086	176.174
21	23	4	Jimmy Spencer	Winston Ford	51.123	176.046
22	13	3	W. Dallenbach Jr.	First Plus Ford	51.149	175.957
23	81	3	Kenny Wallace	Square D Ford	51.174	175.871
24	4	4	Bobby Hamilton	Kodak Film Chevy	51.175	175.867
25	1	0	Steve Park	Pennzoil Chevy	51.196	175.795
26	41	2	Steve Grissom	Kodiak Chevy	51.201	175.778
27	10	4	Ricky Rudd	Tide/Whirlpool Ford	51.209	175.750
28	3	4	Dale Earnhardt	GM Goodwrench Chevy	51.233	175.668
29	21	4	Michael Waltrip	CITGO Petroleum Ford	51.268	175.548
30	22	4	Ward Burton	MBNA America Pontiac	51.285	175.490
31	98	3	Rich Bickle	Thorn Apple Valley Ford	51.325	175.353
32	71	3	Dave Marcis	Realtree Chevy	51.389	175.135
33	44	4	Kyle Petty	Hot Wheels Pontiac	51.423	175.019
34	99	4	Jeff Burton	Exide Batteries Ford	51.458	174.900
35	97	1	Chad Little	John Deere Ford	51.463	174.883
36	91	3	Morgan Shepherd	Little Joe's Chevy	51.511	174.720
37	94	4	Bill Elliott	McDonald's Ford	Provisional	
38	16	4	Ted Musgrave	Primestar Ford	Provisional	
39	26	2	Johnny Benson Jr.	Cheerios Ford	Provisional	
40	11	4	Brett Bodine	Paychex Ford	Provisional	
41	9	0	Jerry Nadeau	Cartoon Network Ford	Provisional	
42	75	4	Rick Mast	Remington Arms Ford	Provisional	
43	35	4	Darrell Waltrip	Tabasco Chevy	Provisional	

* New track record: Old mark, 177.736 mph by Ernie Irvan on July 31, 1997
1998 36 Car Qualifying Average: 176.445 mph
1997 38 Car Qualifying Average: 175.663 mph
Difference: +0.782 mph

Field by Make of Car: Chevy - 16 • Ford - 22 • Pontiac - 5